Vocabulary Drills

Jamestown's Reading Improvement

Edward B. Fry, Ph.D.

JAMESTOWN EDUCATION

Acknowledgments

Acknowledgment is gratefully made to the following publishers, authors, and agents for permission to reprint these works. Every effort has been made to determine copyright owners. In the case of any omissions, the Publishers will be pleased to make suitable acknowledgments in future editions.

"Whatever Happened to the Mayflower?" adapted from "Old Cricket Says." Reprinted by permission of CRICKET magazine, November 1998, Vol. 26, No. 3, © 1998 by Carus Publishing Company.

"Take Me Out to the Ball Game" adapted from "Old Cricket Says." Reprinted by permission of CRICKET magazine, July 1997, Vol. 24, No. 11, © 1997 by Carus Publishing Company.

"Glaciers on the Move" adapted from "Glaciers on the Move" from GLACIERS, by Roy A. Gallant. Copyright © 1999 by Roy A. Gallant. Reprinted by permission of Grolier Publishing Company.

"Trudy Ederle's Swim of a Lifetime" adapted from "America's Best Girl" by Tracey E. Fern. Copyright © 2001 by Highlights for Children, Inc., Columbus, OH.

"The Old Oaken Bucket" adapted from "The Old Oaken Bucket" by Edmund A. Fortier. Copyright © 2000 by Highlights for Children, Inc., Columbus, OH.

"The Wandering Albatross" adapted from "Tracking the Wandering Albatross" by Jack Myers. Copyright © 2001 by Highlights for Children, Inc., Columbus, OH.

"Albert Comes Home" adapted from ODYSSEY's October 2000 issue: "Albert Comes Home," © 2000, Cobblestone Publishing Company, 30 Grove Street, Suite C, Peterborough, NH 03458. All Rights Reserved. Reprinted by permission of the publisher.

Cover Design: Lightbourne

Glencoe/McGraw-Hill

A Division of The McGraw-Hill Companies

Send all inquiries to:
Glencoe/McGraw-Hill
130 E. Randolph Street
Suite 400
Chicago, IL 60601

ISBN 0-07-827367-6

Printed in the United States of America.

9 10 DOH 12

Contents

To the Student

Introduction

Why build your vocabulary?

The aim of *Vocabulary Drills* is to help you learn how to approach new words and to become more comfortable with the language—free to explore new words and their meanings. In this book you will work with useful vocabulary that is presented in reading selections on many subjects and from many different types of sources. As you read the selections and do the exercises that accompany them, you will be developing your skills in dealing with new words—skills that you can carry over to your own reading.

Using Context

One of the most important skills you will learn is using context to help you get some idea of the meaning of an unfamiliar word. Context is the setting of the word—the ideas in the words and sentences that surround it. A word in a sentence carries an idea that fits in with the meaning of the whole sentence and of the paragraph in which the sentence is located.

When you are reading on your own and come across an unfamiliar word, you don't usually want to stop reading to check for the meaning of the word in a dictionary. You should just try to get a fair sense of the word's meaning from its context and keep on reading. You can often come quite close to the meaning of a word by making a guess at it, on the basis of the context. That is a skill you will develop as you use this book.

Learning Vocabulary Skills

Another way that people build their vocabularies is by learning how words are formed and how words are related to one another. The Word Study lessons will help you learn the meanings of some Greek and Latin roots and some words that contain those roots. The Word Study lessons will also show you how some words have more than one meaning. They will also give you practice in using analogies, synonyms, and figures of speech to help you understand word meanings.

How to Use This Book

Vocabulary Drills is divided into 28 lessons. Every fifth lesson is a Review and Extension lesson that provides additional work with the words and skills introduced in the four lessons preceding it.

The ideal way to approach the lessons and exercises is to work through the exercises on your own. Then, if possible, correct your answers in a group with classmates, using the Answer Key provided by your teacher. Using words aloud and hearing them spoken helps to make them a part of your vocabulary. Talking about the words and discussing the answers to the exercises will help you better understand the words and how they are used.

Meeting Words in Context

Each of these odd-numbered lessons begins with a short reading passage that contains vocabulary words you will work with in the lessons. The passages are taken from many kinds of reading material, including newspapers, magazines, fiction and nonfiction, textbooks, and reference materials.

The five vocabulary words in each passage appear in boldfaced type. As you read a passage, try to figure out the meanings of the boldfaced words from the way they are used. Pay close attention to the ideas contained in the words and sentences that surround each vocabulary word. Try to understand how the vocabulary word fits in with those ideas.

The reading passage is followed by a Personal Words section. Here you write two words from the passage—*not* the boldfaced words—whose meanings you are not sure of. Make a guess at the meaning of each word, and write that meaning beside the word. Then at the end of the lesson, in the Personal Words Follow-up, compare your definition with one from a dictionary. Check to see how close your definition came to the one given in the dictionary. Finally, enter your two words and their correct definitions on the Personal Words pages that begin on page 108.

Four exercises follow each reading passage. In these exercises you will explore the meanings of the five vocabulary words as they are used in the passage. There are three types of exercises—multiple choice, word substitution, and fill in the blanks.

The exercises called Using Context ask you to try to figure out the meanings of the words from the way they are used in the passage. In Making Connections you substitute synonyms and antonyms for the words, substitute their definitions for the words, or use the words to complete sentences or analogies.

Word Study

In each of the even-numbered lessons, an introduction teaches a skill that will help you discover how words are formed or how words relate to one another. Following are three exercises in which you work with the skill that was introduced. The exercises contain word-substitution, fill-in-the-blank, matching, and multiple-choice questions.

Review and Extension

The five exercises in this section build on your understanding of the words you have worked with in the preceding lessons.

Checking Your Work

Personal Words. Write your own new vocabulary words in the Personal Words section on pages 108–112. Once you have recorded words and their definitions on these pages, read them over from time to time to make them part of your everyday writing and communicating.

Glossary. All of the vocabulary words, their pronunciations, and their definitions are contained in the glossary on pages 113–121. Be sure when you consult the glossary that if more than one definition is given for a word, you choose the one that has the meaning you are looking for.

Answer Key. Check your work by referring to the answer key provided by your teacher. Try to figure out why the correct answer was correct. If you are confused by an answer, discuss it with the other members of the group or with your teacher. Remember, your main goal is to develop your ability to learn and use words.

Word and Word Part List. The alphabetical Word and Word Part List on pages 122–124 is a handy reference that tells you which lesson introduced each vocabulary word.

Remember that the more words you know, the better you will understand what you read and the better you will be able to communicate. Good luck!

1 | Spiders and the Silky Threads They Spin

Do you like spiders? Many people do not. These people think of spiders as being creepy insects. Actually spiders are not insects at all. They are animals that just **resemble** insects.

Spiders belong to the class of animals called arachnids. This class also includes scorpions. There are many families and several kinds of spiders. Some **authorities** think there are more than 40,000 varieties of spiders.

Spiders are known for the silky webs they can spin, or weave. In summertime you have probably seen beautifully shaped spider webs. They are especially beautiful in the early morning when covered with dew. The morning sun makes the webs glisten.

Some spiders use their webs to help them **obtain** food. Insects are caught on the web threads, which the spider has smeared with a sticky material. A spider knows when an insect has been caught because a signal line runs from the web to the spider. The spider then ties up its **prey** with thread and carries it away to be eaten or stored.

All spiders can make the silky threads used to spin webs. But not all spiders spin webs. Some use their web threads to make homes or web nests. Others live inside tunnel-like webs. Still others **dwell** in underground dens lined with silky threads. Water spiders live at the bottom of ponds in homes made of waterproof web threads.

Spiders use their threads in many ways. The raft-spider travels over water on leaves and twigs tied together by its web threads. Some spiders can spin threads to use as a bridge to cross small streams.

Personal Words

Choose two words from the selection that are not familiar to you or whose meanings you are not completely sure of. (Do not choose words that appear in boldfaced type.) Write the words on the lines provided. Beside each word write what you think it means, according to how it was used in the selection.

1. _____ : _____

    _____

2. _____ : _____

    _____

4

Using Context

A Put an **X** in the box beside the correct meaning for each boldfaced word. For clues to the meanings of the words, reread the parts of the passage in which they appear.

1. Spiders are animals that just **resemble** insects.
   - ☐ a. pretend to be like
   - ☐ b. are similar to
   - ☐ c. are the same size as

2. Some **authorities** think there are more than 40,000 varieties of spiders.
   - ☐ a. police officers
   - ☐ b. books about spiders
   - ☐ c. experts on some subject

3. Spiders use their silky, sticky webs to help them **obtain** food.
   - ☐ a. get
   - ☐ b. give away
   - ☐ c. plant

4. The spider ties up its **prey** with thread and carries it away.
   - ☐ a. animal hunted for food
   - ☐ b. a sticky material
   - ☐ c. silky thread

5. Some spiders **dwell** in underground dens lined with silky threads.
   - ☐ a. dig
   - ☐ b. live
   - ☐ c. hide

B Circle the correct meaning for each vocabulary word. Then write the word in a sentence on the line provided. For clues to the meanings of the words, reread the parts of the passage in which they appear.

1. **resemble**	be different	be able	be like	be ready

2. **authorities**	beginners	laws	experts	citizens

3. **obtain**	gain	refuse	cover up	ask for

4. **prey**	tropical fish	hunter	wild bird	hunted animal

5. **dwell**	build	live in	wander	invent

Making Connections

A On the line beside each sentence, write the vocabulary word that has the same meaning as the underlined word or words.

resemble   authorities   obtain   prey   dwell

1. _____ The <u>hunted zebra</u> tried to outrun the hungry tiger, but the tiger was too fast.

2. _____ Sam wondered how Fred was able to <u>get possession of</u> a new bike.

3. _____ <u>Experts</u> from the state capital will be called in to help solve our town's traffic problems.

4. _____ Some North American Indians used to <u>live</u> in tents called tepees.

5. _____ Spiders are not insects, but they <u>are similar to</u> insects in some ways.

B Complete each sentence with the correct vocabulary word.

resemble   authorities   obtain   prey   dwell

1. The school _____ ended classes today because of the storm.

2. Students must _____ permission to leave school.

3. Kelvin and Cory _____ each other, but they are not brothers.

4. Thousands of bats _____ in the caves in that mountain.

5. Our cat almost caught a mouse, but the _____ got away.

Personal Words Follow-up

Use a dictionary to help you find the definitions for the personal words you chose at the beginning of this lesson. If a word has more than one meaning, look for the meaning that defines the word as it is used in the selection. Then write the words and their dictionary definitions in the Personal Words pages at the back of the book.

2 | Word Study: Context Clues

Sometimes in your reading you will come to a word that you don't know. For example, read the following sentences carefully:

Megan visited the Franklin Park Zoo yesterday. She was amazed at the many kinds of **fauna** she saw there. She especially liked seeing the kangaroos and the bear-like koalas from Australia.

Perhaps you have never seen or heard the boldfaced word *fauna* before. When you come to a word in your reading that you don't know, the context may help you figure out its meaning. The context—the words or sentences before and after the unknown word—often give clues to the word's meaning.

Notice that the first sentence tells you that Megan visited a zoo. Why do people usually go to a zoo? Yes, they go to see interesting animals. The third sentence tells you that Megan enjoyed seeing the kangaroos and the koalas. Are they animals? What do you think the word *fauna* means? Yes, it means "animals." You were able to figure out the meaning of the word by using context clues. When you come to a word you don't know, try using context clues to figure out a meaning that makes sense in what you are reading.

Finding Meanings

Put an **X** in the box beside the correct meaning for each boldfaced word. Use the context to help you.

1. The storm had become worse. The trip down the mountain would be **perilous**.
    - ☐ a. very fast
    - ☐ b. full of danger
    - ☐ c. quite safe

2. It's hard to believe Ed was once so **frail**. Now he is our best soccer player.
    - ☐ a. smart
    - ☐ b. strong
    - ☐ c. weak

3. The little mouse was **wary**. He knew the family cat was in the house.
    - ☐ a. careless
    - ☐ b. tired
    - ☐ c. careful

4. Our dog **pursued** the neighbor's cat, but the cat got away from her.
    - ☐ a. chased
    - ☐ b. played with
    - ☐ c. barked at

5. The storm raged all night. But early the next morning, it began to **subside**.
    - ☐ a. quiet down
    - ☐ b. get stronger
    - ☐ c. turn to rain

Sense and Meaning

Three meanings are given for the boldfaced word in each sentence.
Use the context to help you decide which meaning makes the
most sense in that sentence. Then circle the correct meaning.

1. The mule was so **obstinate** that he wouldn't do anything Ami asked him to do.

    strong   helpful   stubborn

2. Pedro's dog suddenly howled out in pain. She had stepped on a sharp thorn. Pedro
    held the dog's paw firmly while he **extracted** the thorn.

    pulled out   pushed in   cleaned

3. Ted felt **panicky**. While hiking in the woods, he realized that he was lost!

    relieved   very angry   full of fear

4. The captain of the fishing boat checked the boat's **provisions**. Fishing was hard
    work. She knew that the crew would be very hungry and thirsty each day.

    fishing poles   fuel supply   supply of food and drink

5. Most family pets, such as cats and dogs, are **domestic** animals. Wild animals, such as
    foxes and coyotes, would not make good pets for the home.

    tame   expensive   unfriendly

Making Connections

The words listed below are vocabulary words you studied in this
lesson. Complete each sentence with the correct word. If you
are unsure of the meaning of a word, look it up in the glossary.

wary	pursued	subside	obstinate	extracted

1. The police officers _____ the bank robber's car.

2. Nancy's aching tooth had to be _____ by the dentist.

3. If the rain does not _____ , the river will flood the town.

4. The firemen were _____ about entering the burning barn.

5. Grandpa was _____ and wouldn't accept our help.

3 | Strange Animals of Australia

Australia is known as the world's smallest continent. This island continent is also known for its many unusual animals. These animals are not found living naturally anywhere else in the world.

Perhaps the most **remarkable** of these animals is the platypus. It has fur like a beaver's and a bill like a duck's. It also has wide webbed feet. Even though the platypus is a mammal, it lays eggs like a bird!

The kangaroo is the best known of Australia's animals. There are many **species** of kangaroos. The smallest kangaroo is the wallaby. It is only as big as a rabbit. The largest kangaroo is more than seven feet tall. Kangaroos carry their babies in pouches until the babies are able to move about by themselves. Kangaroos have strong hind legs and powerful tails, which help them to leap along the ground as fast as 25 miles an hour.

One of Australia's most popular animals is the koala. It looks like a teddy bear, but it is not really a bear. Like kangaroos, koalas carry their babies in pouches. As baby koalas get a little older, they ride on their mothers' backs. Koalas live in trees. A strange sight is to see koalas **suspended** upside down from the branches of a tree. They seem to enjoy being in that position.

Another unusual animal is one that is not popular at all. It is the dingo, the wild dog of Australia. Dingoes look like small wolves. Dingoes **differ** in color, ranging from black to yellowish-white. They hunt alone or in packs. They often kill small kangaroos and sheep. No wonder the sheep ranchers **detest** dingoes.

The animals of Australia, like the continent itself, are unusual—but very interesting.

Personal Words

Choose two words from the selection that are not familiar to you or whose meaning you are not completely sure of. (Do not choose words that appear in boldfaced type.) Write the words on the lines provided. Beside each word write what you think it means, according to how it was used in the selection.

1. _____ : _____

_____

2. _____ : _____

_____

Using Context

A Put an **X** in the box beside the correct meaning for each boldfaced word. For clues to the meanings of the words, reread the parts of the passage in which they appear.

1. Describing the platypus as a **remarkable** animal means that you think it is
   - ☐ a. ordinary.
   - ☐ b. dangerous.
   - ☐ c. unusual.

2. If scientists discovered two new **species** of birds, they discovered two new
   - ☐ a. kinds of birds.
   - ☐ b. enemies of birds.
   - ☐ c. nesting places of birds.

3. The sentence in which the word **suspended** appears helps you understand that in this context *suspended* means
   - ☐ a. climbing.
   - ☐ b. falling.
   - ☐ c. hanging.

4. If a group of birds **differ** in color, the colors of the birds
   - ☐ a. are alike.
   - ☐ b. vary.
   - ☐ c. are dull.

5. From the context in which the word **detest** appears, you can tell that if the sheepranchers *detest* dingoes, they
   - ☐ a. like the dingoes.
   - ☐ b. hate the dingoes.
   - ☐ c. round up the dingoes.

B Go back and read the paragraph in which each boldfaced word appears. Pay special attention to the sentence in which it is used. Then circle the word that has the same or almost the same meaning.

1. **remarkable**	popular	unusual	famous	familiar
2. **species**	enemy	color	type	name
3. **suspended**	attached	hung	carried	separated
4. **differ**	agree	argue	remain	vary
5. **detest**	dislike	favor	disturb	protect

Making Connections

A On the line beside each word or phrase, write the vocabulary
word that is related to it. The related word or phrase may
have the same or a similar meaning as the vocabulary word.
Or it may have an opposite meaning.

> **remarkable**   **species**   **suspended**   **differ**   **detest**

1. type _____   6. class _____

2. be fond of _____   7. special _____

3. hanging down _____   8. love _____

4. are the same _____   9. are unlike _____

5. common _____   10. held up _____

B Complete each sentence with the correct vocabulary word.

> **remarkable**   **species**   **suspended**   **differ**   **detest**

1. The boys on the basketball team may _____ in height, but
they are all good players.

2. Ray's kite got caught in the tree, and now it's _____ from a
branch.

3. Sarah's display of 10 _____ of butterflies won her a second
prize at the school science fair.

4. Many people _____ the cold and snow of winter, but many others
love this season of the year.

5. White sharks, growing to a length of 20 to 30 feet, are _____ fish.

Personal Words Follow-up

Use a dictionary to help you find the definitions for the
personal words you chose at the beginning of this lesson. If a
word has more than one meaning, look for the meaning that
defines the word as it is used in the selection. Then write the
words and their dictionary definitions in the Personal Words
pages at the back of the book.

4 | Word Study: Multiple Meaning Words

Sometimes in your reading you come to a word that has more than one meaning. For example, read the following sentences:

1. My sister Audrey is in the fifth **grade**.
2. Tom's **grade** on his spelling test was 95.
3. Pedaling my bicycle up the steep **grade** was hard.

   In each sentence the word *grade* has a different meaning. In one it means "the mark one receives for schoolwork." In another it means "the slope of a road." In another it means "a class in school." How do you know which meaning fits each sentence? In lesson 2 you learned that the context could help you figure out the meaning of an unknown word. You can also use the context to help you decide which of several meanings of a word is the correct one.

   Which meaning of *grade* makes sense in sentence 1? Yes, "a class in school" makes sense. Which meaning makes sense in sentence 2? In that sentence *grade* means "the mark one receives for schoolwork." Which meaning makes sense in sentence 3? Yes, in that sentence *grade* means the "slope of a road." Remember—the context often gives you clues to the correct meaning of a word.

Finding Meanings

The boldfaced word in each sentence below has three meanings.
Put an **X** in the box beside the meaning that makes the most sense.

1. Debbie knew that Jill would never **break** her promise to her.
   - ☐ a. come apart
   - ☐ b. fail to keep
   - ☐ c. train to obey

2. Manny didn't want to be seen, so he tried to **slip** out of the room.
   - ☐ a. slide suddenly
   - ☐ b. move quietly
   - ☐ c. make a mistake

3. Mother stored all my class pictures in a **trunk** in the attic.
   - ☐ a. a big box for holding things
   - ☐ b. the main stem of a tree
   - ☐ c. the long snout of an elephant

4. Tino lost his **balance** and almost fell off the ladder.
   - ☐ a. instrument for weighing
   - ☐ b. amount that is left over
   - ☐ c. steady position

5. Dad went out in his boat, but we decided to fish from the **bank**.
   - ☐ a. ground bordering a river or lake
   - ☐ b. place where money is kept
   - ☐ c. a long pile or heap

Sense and Meaning

Three meanings are given for the boldfaced word in each
sentence. Use the context to help you decide which meaning
makes the most sense in that sentence. Then circle the correct
meaning.

1. Andy was surprised to learn that he had gained a **pound** since yesterday.

    hit heavily   unit of weight   place for stray animals

2. The leaves on the trees are a **blaze** of color during the fall season.

    bright fire   mark made on a tree   bright display

3. At night we could hear the sad **bay** of a dog across the lake.

    part of a sea   reddish-brown horse   long, deep barking

4. Caryn tied the pony to the fence **post**.

    upright support   job or position   system for mail delivery

5. Last spring we had an unusual **spell** of bad weather that lasted for two weeks.

    period of work   period of time   magic charm

Making Connections

The words listed below are vocabulary words you studied in this
lesson. Complete each sentence with the correct word. Use the
context of each sentence to help you.

   trunk   balance   blaze   bay   post

1. Ahmad saved half of his allowance and spent the _____.

2. Anna hoped to ride her _____ in the jumping contest.

3. We sent the packages to my grandmother by _____.

4. The hurricane uprooted the _____ of our big oak tree.

5. When the firemen arrived, the _____ was out of control.

1-4 | Review and Extension

Finding Meanings

A The boldfaced words listed below are vocabulary words you studied in lessons 1 and 3. Match each word with its meaning by writing the letter of the meaning beside each word.

_____ 1. **prey**   a. an animal hunted and killed for food

_____ 2. **differ**   b. a kind or type; class

_____ 3. **obtain**   c. hanging down; held in place

_____ 4. **suspended**   d. to be unlike; to vary

_____ 5. **species**   e. to get; to gain

B The boldfaced words listed below are words you studied in lesson 4. Two meanings of each word are given. Match each word with its two meanings by writing the letters of the meanings beside each word.

_____ 1. **bay**   a. the ground bordering a river or lake

_____   b. a steady position

_____ 2. **slip**   c. a system for mail delivery

_____   d. a reddish-brown horse

_____ 3. **balance**   e. to move quietly

_____   f. a place where money is kept

_____ 4. **post**   g. the amount that is left over

_____   h. an upright support

_____ 5. **bank**   i. a part of a sea

_____   j. to make a mistake

Sense and Meaning

The boldfaced word in each incomplete sentence below is a word you studied in lesson 2. Complete each sentence so that it makes sense and shows the meaning of the boldfaced word.

1. The cows in the middle of the road were so **obstinate**, they _____

   _____

2. It would be **perilous** to try to cross the ice-covered lake because _____

   _____

3. Dogs and cats are **domestic** animals, unlike _____

   _____

4. The noise in the school lunchroom began to **subside** when _____

   _____

5. When he saw that Dan was **panicky** about the book report, Paul _____

   _____

6. Even though my grandfather is **frail**, he can still _____

   _____

7. Liz knew that her tooth would have to be **extracted**, so she _____

   _____

8. The mother deer became **wary** when she saw _____

   _____

9. The runaway horse was **pursued** by several cowboys who _____

   _____

10. Unless the explorers could find some **provisions** soon, they _____

    _____

Synonym Study

A *synonym* is a word that has the same or nearly the same meaning as another word. Following are synonym studies for two vocabulary words you studied in lessons 1 and 3. Use either the vocabulary words or their synonyms to complete the sentences in this exercise. Check with the synonym studies as you decide which choice best fits the context of each sentence.

dwell   **reside**   **occupy**

The words *dwell, reside,* and *occupy* all mean "to live" or "to live in." *Dwell* is generally used when talking about where one makes a home. *Some desert people dwell in tents. Reside* is usually a stronger or more formal word and means "to live in or at for a long time" or "to live officially in a place." *The king and queen reside in the palace.* If you occupy a place, you are actually in it. *Two families now occupy the house across the street.*

1. During her term in office, the newly elected governor will _____ in the governor's mansion.

2. Troop 105 will _____ the camp's main building for the first three weeks.

3. Thousands of years ago many people use to _____ in caves.

detest   **dislike**

Detest and *dislike* both mean "not to like." *Detest* is a stronger word that means "to not like someone or something very much." *Many people detest spiders. Dislike* is a milder word that suggests not liking something because one doesn't enjoy it or doesn't find it interesting. *My brothers dislike peas and would rather eat carrots.*

4. Most people who _____ soccer don't understand the sport.

5. After weeks of hissing and growling, it's clear that our cat and the

neighbor's new dog _____ one another.

16

Word Forms

The boldfaced words listed below are other forms of the
vocabulary words you studied in lessons 1 and 3. Complete
each sentence with the correct word. If you are unsure of the
meaning of a word, look it up in the glossary.

difference   **obtainable**   **resemblance**   **differently**

detestable   **dwelling**   **authorize**   **suspension**

1. A _____ bridge is one that is hung on cables between two towers.

2. Gary knew that the information he was looking for was not _____ in the local library.

3. The _____ in which Roberta lived when she was young will soon be torn down.

4. Identical twins have a _____ to one another.

5. Many people believe that there is no one more _____ than a person who lies.

6. I like the way you drew those willow trees, but I probably would have drawn them

   _____

7. The principal has to _____ every school poster before it is hung.

8. Kevin didn't think there was much _____ between the two students running for class president.

9. Clean air and water are _____ if people stop polluting.

10. There is a large _____ in price between the two computers that are on sale.

Using Your Vocabulary

The scrambled words in boldface below are vocabulary words you studied in lessons 1 and 3. Rearrange the letters of each word to form its correct spelling. Then use the word to complete the sentence next to it. Be sure that the word makes sense in the sentence. If you need to, look back at the vocabulary words in lessons 1 and 3.

1. **wldel**

2. **urtihatiseo**

3. **bsemelre**

4. **ecsipse**

5. **anotib**

6. **yrep**

7. **larebamker**

8. **refdif**

9. **ensupdesd**

10. **tseetd**

1. Many strange creatures _____ in the Amazon forests.

2. Some _____ on the subject believe that travel in outer space will be common someday.

3. Alligators and crocodiles _____ each other, but alligators have shorter and flatter heads.

4. There are two _____ of alligators, one living in the United States and the other in China.

5. Dave has to _____ his father's permission before he can go to the game.

6. Spotting his _____ in the field below, the hawk dived upon it.

7. The ostrich is a _____ bird that can run fast but cannot fly.

8. When Mother's four rose plants bloom, the flowers of each will _____ in color from the others.

9. We saw several bats _____ from the roof of the deserted barn.

10. The two teams do not _____ each other, but they surely don't like each other.

5 | Violent Storms in the United States

If you don't like the weather, wait for a while. It will change." Have you ever heard that old saying or one like it? It is certainly an **accurate** saying. Our weather changes day by day. One day it's warm and sunny. The next day it's cool and cloudy. Then some days a storm moves in and brings with it nasty weather, such as rain or snow.

Some kinds of storms that occur in the United States are worse than nasty. They are storms that bring **violent** weather. Tornadoes are the most violent of these storms. They produce winds of **incredible** force. Their twisting winds can reach speeds of more than 120 miles an hour. Tornadoes look like funnel-shaped dark clouds. As they twist along, they leave a path of **destruction**. They pull up trees and tear up the ground. They smash or carry away buildings.

Hurricanes are the biggest of our violent storms. They can be more than 400 miles wide. Their powerful winds can reach speeds of 125 miles an hour. Such winds blow down trees and wreck power lines. Along the shore, they can cause huge waves that carry away boats and buildings.

Blizzards are heavy snowstorms with very strong winds. They **hinder** travel by blocking roads and train routes with huge snowdrifts. They make it impossible for airplanes to fly.

Thunderstorms are the most common of our violent storms. They can cause much damage. Some of the damage is caused by heavy rains, which can wash soil away and produce flooding. Some is caused by lightning, which can set fire to buildings and forests.

Our weather is always changing. We can only hope that our violent storms are few and far between.

Personal Words

Choose two words from the selection that are not familiar to you or whose meanings you are not completely sure of. (Do not choose words that appear in boldfaced type.) Write the words on the lines provided. Beside each word write what you think it means, according to how it was used in the selection.

1. _____ : _____

_____

2. _____ : _____

_____

Using Context

A For each vocabulary word, put an **X** in the box beside its correct meaning. Try to figure out what the word means from the way it is used in the selection.

1. **accurate**
   - ☐ a. important
   - ☐ b. exactly right
   - ☐ c. not correct

2. **violent**
   - ☐ a. mostly pleasant
   - ☐ b. with uncontrolled force
   - ☐ c. without warning

3. **incredible**
   - ☐ a. unbelievable
   - ☐ b. movable
   - ☐ c. usual

4. **destruction**
   - ☐ a. repair
   - ☐ b. shelter
   - ☐ c. great damage

5. **hinder**
   - ☐ a. stop
   - ☐ b. increase
   - ☐ c. speed up

B Write each vocabulary word beside its meaning. To figure out what each word means, go back to the passage and read the sentence that contains the word. If you can't discover the meaning from the way the word is used in the sentence, look for clues in the sentences that come before and after it.

accurate	violent	incredible	destruction	hinder

1. _____ to cause delay

2. _____ acting with strong force

3. _____ condition of being destroyed

4. _____ correct

5. _____ hard to believe

Making Connections

A Complete each sentence with the correct vocabulary word.

accurate	violent	incredible	destruction	hinder

1. The earthquake caused great _____ in the small village.

2. The shortage of water will _____ the firemen's efforts to put out the fire.

3. The librarian was certain that her count of the books was _____.

4. Modern jet planes can fly at _____ speeds.

5. The _____ sea put the small ship in danger of sinking.

B On the line beside each word, write the vocabulary word that is related to it. The related word may be a synonym, an antonym, or a definition for the vocabulary word.

accurate	violent	incredible	destruction	hinder

1. peaceful _____

2. delay _____

3. common _____

4. ruins _____

5. correct _____

6. hurry _____

7. raging _____

8. wrong _____

9. stop _____

10. unbelievable _____

Personal Words Follow-up

Use a dictionary to help you find the definitions for the personal words you chose at the beginning of this lesson. If a word has more than one meaning, look for the meaning that defines the word as it is used in the selection. Then write the words and their dictionary definitions in the Personal Words pages at the back of the book.

6 | Word Study: Noun and Verb Meanings

The word *grade* has many meanings. In sentence 1 it means "the mark one receives for schoolwork." In sentence 2 it means "the slope of a road." In both sentences, *grade* is used as a noun (a word that names a person, place, or thing).

1. Tom's **grade** on the spelling test was 95.
2. Pedaling my bicycle up the steep **grade** was hard.

Many words can be used as more than one part of speech. For example, *grade* can also be used as a verb (a word that shows action).

3. Our teacher will **grade** our tests tonight.
4. The workers will **grade** the bumpy dirt road.

In sentence 3 the verb *grade* means "to give a rating mark for a student's work." In sentence 4 it means "to make smooth or level."

Remember, many words have more than one meaning. And some words have both noun meanings and verb meanings.

Finding Meanings

A noun and a verb meaning are given for the boldfaced word in each sentence. Circle the meaning that is used in the sentence. Then write N for noun meaning or V for verb meaning on the line beside each sentence.

_____ 1. Tomo had to **duck** under the low branch.

large wild bird   lower the head suddenly

_____ 2. It's time to **light** the candles on Mom's birthday cake.

brightness   cause to burn

_____ 3. The tug's **wake** almost sank our small boat.

stop sleeping   trail left by a ship

_____ 4. Patrice could not **match** Nguyen's bowling score.

be equal to   stick used to light fires

_____ 5. The lion tamer's **lash** stung the growling lion.

tie or fasten   cord part of a whip

Sense and Meaning

Three meanings are given for the boldfaced word in each sentence. Both noun and verb meanings are given. Use the context to help you decide which meaning makes the most sense in that sentence. Then circle the correct meaning.

1. Washing **pitch** off your hands is very hard to do.

    fall forward   sticky tar   throw something

2. The power outage caused my computer to **crash**.

    sudden loud noise   fall or break   fail to work

3. It's not good for anyone to **harbor** feelings of anger.

    give shelter   shelter for ships   keep in the mind

4. The **play** was so bad that we left after the first act.

    story acted out   turn in a game   have fun

5. How many fish did you **catch** yesterday?

    ball game   take or get hold of   surprise

Making Connections

The words listed below are vocabulary words you studied in this lesson. Complete each sentence with the correct word. Use the context of each sentence to help you.

light   **wake**   **pitch**   **crash**   **harbor**

1. The fishing boats stayed in the _____ until the storm passed.

2. Rob was so tired that I didn't _____ him until 10:00.

3. Three people died in the _____ on the highway.

4. The _____ at the top of the stairs burned out.

5. Cassie hoped to _____ in the All-Star Game.

7 | Should You Help a Fledgling?

One early summer day my son and I were walking in the woods. Suddenly we came across a lone baby bird lying on the ground. It was fluttering all about. It flapped its tiny wings furiously, but it could not fly. I could see that it had just begun to grow its feathers. It was a fledgling. The tiny bird looked frightened and helpless.

My son thought that we should take the bird home and try to raise it. Is that what you would do? There are several reasons why that might not be a good idea.

You would need to be **cautious** about what you fed the bird. You would have to find out what its natural food is. Some birds eat only seeds. Others eat only live insects. Many eat worms. Once you have the right food, you'd have to feed the fledgling every hour. It would open its mouth, waiting for you to drop its food in.

A fledgling found fluttering about on the ground may not need your **assistance**. Chances are good that the mother is close by, managing her fledgling's first flying lesson. She is probably **concealed** in a nearby bush or tree. If you keep quiet and listen, you may hear her calling to her baby. If you stand at a distance, you may even see the mother bird fly down to her baby and give it the help it needs.

Unless you see **evidence** that the mother bird is gone, you should leave the fledgling alone. You should not even touch it. You can be **confident** that the mother bird will take good care of it.

Personal Words

Choose two words from the selection that are not familiar to you or whose meanings you are not completely sure of. (Do not choose words that appear in boldfaced type.) Write the words on the lines provided. Beside each word write what you think it means, according to how it was used in the selection.

1. _____ : _____

_____

2. _____ : _____

_____

Using Context

A Put an **X** in the box beside the correct meaning for each
boldfaced word. For clues to the meanings of the words,
reread the parts of the passage in which they appear.

1. You need to be **cautious** about what
   you feed a fledgling.
   - ☐ a. careless
   - ☐ b. kind
   - ☐ c. careful

2. A fledgling may not need your
   assistance if its mother is nearby.
   - ☐ a. help
   - ☐ b. attention
   - ☐ c. food

3. The mother bird is probably
   concealed in a nearby bush or tree.
   - ☐ a. hidden
   - ☐ b. lost
   - ☐ c. asleep

4. Unless you see **evidence** that the
   mother bird is gone, do not try to
   help the fledgling.
   - ☐ a. reason
   - ☐ b. sign
   - ☐ c. sorrow

5. You can be **confident** that the mother
   bird will take good care of the fledgling.
   - ☐ a. surprised
   - ☐ b. doubtful
   - ☐ c. sure

B Circle the correct meaning for each vocabulary word. Then write the
word in a sentence on the line provided. For clues to the meanings
of the words, reread the parts of the passage in which they appear.

1. **cautious**	worried	careful	thoughtful	foolish

2. **assistance**	directions	warning	aid	control

3. **concealed**	nesting	clearly seen	trapped	out of sight

4. **evidence**	feathers	sorrow	facts	worry

5. **confident**	certain	concerned	unsure	happy

Making Connections

A On the line beside each sentence, write the vocabulary word that has the same meaning as the underlined word or words.

cautious	assistance	concealed	evidence	confident

1. _____ Mom kept Dad's birthday present <u>out of sight</u> so that he wouldn't see it.

2. _____ The police could find no <u>sign</u> that the house had been broken into.

3. _____ Ellen was <u>very careful</u> as she walked across the icy surface of the pond.

4. _____ Alex was <u>sure</u> that his team would be able to win its next game.

5. _____ The Red Cross provides <u>aid</u> to people in need of help.

B Write each vocabulary word on the line beside the synonym and antonym.

cautious	assistance	concealed	evidence	confident

	Synonym	Antonym
1. _____	hidden	found
2. _____	help	harm
3. _____	certain	doubtful
4. _____	proof	(no antonym)
5. _____	careful	careless

Personal Words Follow-up

Use a dictionary to help you find the definitions for the personal words you chose at the beginning of this lesson. If a word has more than one meaning, look for the meaning that defines the word as it is used in the selection. Then write the words and their dictionary definitions in the Personal Words pages at the back of the book.

8 | Word Study: Compound Words

A compound word is a word made up of two smaller words. The boldfaced words below are compound words.

mailbox   **paintbrush**   **toothache**

The word *mailbox* is made up of the two smaller words *mail* and *box*. The word *paintbrush* is made up of the words *paint* and *brush*. What two words make up the compound word *toothache*?

Studying the two words that make up a compound word can help you understand the meaning of the compound word. For example, a mailbox is a box into which mail is put. A paintbrush is a brush for putting on paint. What is a toothache?

Study each boldfaced word to see whether it is a compound word. If it is, use the meanings of the two words that make up the compound word to help you understand its meaning.

grapevine   **checkbook**   **rancher**   **lawbreaker**

Did you identify *grapevine, checkbook,* and *lawbreaker* as the compound words? You can use the meanings of the smaller words in each compound word to help you figure out its meaning. A grapevine is a vine that grapes grow on. A checkbook is a book containing blank checks. A lawbreaker is someone who breaks the law.

You will often come to a word that may not look familiar to you at first. Study the word carefully to see whether it may be made up of two smaller words you know. It could be a compound word.

Finding Meanings

Complete each sentence with the correct compound word.

| timetable | watchdog | handmade | lifeguard | shipwreck |

1. The big gray _____ began to bark when we approached the gate.

2. The _____ made everyone get out of the water because the waves were so high.

3. Anya looked at the _____ to see when the next train would leave.

4. Tim reported that the _____ was caused by a storm at sea.

5. My aunt gave me a beautiful _____ sweater for my birthday.

Sense and Meaning

Rewrite each sentence on the line provided, using a compound word to replace the underlined phrase.

1. Jason's job was to clean the <u>room where all the supplies were stored</u>.

   _____

2. Kendra wears glasses because of her poor <u>ability to see</u>.

   _____

3. The <u>paved path where people walk</u> is cracked and crumbling.

   _____

4. The <u>marks made by feet</u> in the snow told us that the hunters had come this way.

   _____

5. There is a <u>machine that washes dishes</u> in our new apartment.

   _____

Making Connections

The words listed below are compound words. Complete each sentence with the compound word that makes the most sense.

homesick   sunburn   driftwood   daybreak   skyscraper

1. If you lie outside on a sunny day, you may get a _____.

2. Pieces of wood that are washed ashore from the sea are called _____.

3. A very tall building is sometimes called a _____.

4. The time each morning when daylight first appears is called _____.

5. People away from home for a long time may become _____.

5-8 Review and Extension

Finding Meanings

A Some of the vocabulary words you studied in lessons 5 and 7 have more than one meaning. Complete each sentence with the correct vocabulary word from the list below. In these sentences, the words have meanings different from those they had in the selection. If you are unsure of the different meanings of a word, look it up in the glossary.

violent	concealed	destruction	confident	evidence

1. A crowd gathered to watch the _____ of the old building.

2. After his fall, Laurence experienced some _____ headaches for several days.

3. Ling _____ the truth about her illness from her friends.

4. After hearing all of the _____ in the case, the judge gave his decision.

5. Jerome was _____ that he would win the race.

B The boldfaced words listed below are words you studied in lesson 6. Two meanings of each word are given. One is a noun meaning, and the other is a verb meaning. Match each word with its two meanings by writing the letters of the meanings on the line beside each word.

_____ 1. **lash**   a. to throw something

_____   b. to be equal to

_____ 2. **catch**   c. a ball game

_____   d. a shelter for ships

_____ 3. **pitch**   e. to tie or fasten

_____   f. to keep in mind

_____ 4. **harbor**

_____   —   g. a stick used to light fires

_____   h. to fall forward

_____ 5. **match**   — i. a cord part of a whip

_____   — j. to take or get hold of

Sense and Meaning

Complete each sentence with one of the three compound
words below it. Use the context to help you decide which
compound word makes the most sense in that sentence. Each
of the correct words is a compound you studied in lesson 8.

1. In the days of the early West, the sheriff's job was to arrest any

   _____.

       lawmaker   lawbreaker   lawsuit

2. After a storm, the sea leaves _____ on the beach.

       watercolor   waterfall   driftwood

3. Luis's _____ has improved since he got his new glasses.

       eyebrow   eyelash   eyesight

4. If you take good care of your teeth, you are less likely to have a

   _____.

       toothpaste   toothache   toothpick

5. We found our cat by following its _____ in the sand.

       footballs   foothills   footprints

6. Would you be _____ if you went away to a summer camp?

       homesick   homeless   homeroom

7. The Sears Tower in Chicago is one of the world's tallest _____.

       skylines   skywriters   skyscrapers

8. The deep-sea divers found the _____ at the bottom of the bay.

       shipwreck   shipyard   shipmate

9. A good _____ will bark when a stranger comes near the house.

   watchdog   watchman   watchmaker

10. You must be a strong swimmer if you want to become a _____.

   lifeboat   lifeguard   lifeline

Synonym Study

Following are synonym studies for two vocabulary words you
studied in lessons 5 and 7. Use either the vocabulary words or
their synonyms to complete the sentences in this exercise.
Check with the synonym studies as you decide which choice
best fits the context of each sentence.

evidence   proof

The words *evidence* and *proof* both mean "anything that serves to
show that a belief is true or not true." But there is a slight
difference in meaning between the two words. *Evidence* is used
when speaking of something that is intended to show whether a
belief is true or not true. *The evidence suggests that our dog, Buster,
ate my birthday cake. Proof* is more definite. It is used when speaking
of evidence that is so clear and final that there is no doubt. *The
cake frosting on Buster's face is proof that he ate my birthday cake.*

1. The stolen ring found in the man's pocket was _____ that he
   was guilty.

2. The bread crumbs on the ground were _____ that someone was
   feeding the birds.

destruction   ruins

Destruction and *ruins* both mean "very great damage." *Destruction*,
however, is used when speaking of damage that is so thorough that
it would be impossible to repair. *The firemen's efforts could not prevent
the destruction of the burning building. Ruins* suggests a "falling apart, a
tumbling down, or a rotting away," but it is damage that falls short of
complete destruction. *The ruins of the old wooden bridge could still be seen.*

3. The _____ of the ancient castle attract hundreds of visitors.

4. The _____ caused by the hurricane has made many families
   homeless.

Word Forms

The boldfaced words listed below are other forms of the vocabulary words you studied in lessons 5 and 7. Complete each sentence with the correct word. If you are unsure of the meaning of a word, look it up in the glossary.

evident	**assistant**	**concealing**	**caution**
incredibly	**violence**	**confidence**	**accurately**

1. The lifeguard had to _____ the younger children not to go near the deep end of the pool.

2. Chan won the mile race in the _____ fast time of 4 minutes and 15 seconds.

3. The ocean waves slammed against the sea wall with tremendous

   _____.

4. The heavy rain made it _____ that the soccer game could not be played today.

5. The police arrested the man for _____ evidence of the crime.

6. As a library _____, Anna helps the school librarian in many ways.

7. You must use _____ whenever you climb a tall ladder.

8. Our teacher said that it's more important to do our math work

   _____ than to do it quickly.

9. Manuel was filled with _____ after getting three hits in his first Little League game.

10. The _____ coach manages our team whenever the head coach cannot be at the game.

Using Your Vocabulary

Use vocabulary words introduced in lessons 5–8 to complete
this word puzzle. For each definition or synonym in column A,
think of a vocabulary word that has the same meaning. Then,
in column B, spell out the vocabulary word in the spaces beside
its meaning. One or two letters are provided for each word.

Column A	Column B
1. a sign; proof	__ v __ __ __ n __ __
2. to cause delay; to stop	__ __ __ d __ __
3. exactly right; correct	a __ __ __ __ __ __ e
4. to be equal to	__ __ t __ __
5. mark made by a foot	__ o __ __ __ r __ __ __
6. hidden; out of sight	c __ __ c __ __ __ __ __
7. showing uncontrolled force	__ __ o l __ __ __
8. very careful	__ __ u __ __ __ __ s
9. keep in the mind	h __ __ __ __ __ __
10. aid; help	__ s __ __ __ t __ __ __ __
11. a very tall building	__ k __ __ __ __ __ p __ __
12. caused to burn	__ __ g __ __
13. unbelievable	__ n __ __ __ __ __ b __ __
14. certain; sure	__ __ __ f __ __ __ __ t
15. great damage	d __ __ __ __ u __ __ __ __ __

9 | Whatever Happened to the Mayflower?

Did you ever wonder what happened to the *Mayflower*, the ship that carried 102 Pilgrims to North America in 1620? You might catch a glimpse at a part of the old ship in the Buckinghamshire village of Jordans, England. But don't expect to find the ship docked at a pier. It seems the *Mayflower's* hull may be part of a barn.

In the early 1900s, a historian named Rendel Harris learned that the *Mayflower* had become unseaworthy by 1624 and that the ship's owners had sold its oak timbers. Someone later told Harris that a barn in Jordans had been built from the wood of the *Mayflower*. He started hunting through deeds, wills, and other old papers. He **concluded** that the barn had some real history. He believed it was highly **probable** that the barn's beams had been taken from the ship that had carried the Pilgrims to America.

First, the timbers in the barn had the same age and weight as the timbers of the *Mayflower*. Harris also found evidence that one of the ship's owners had lived in the area where the barn had been **constructed**. The main beam in the barn had a huge crack in it, just like one of the *Mayflower's* beams that had cracked during a storm on its voyage to North America. When Harris examined the beams, the letters *ER HAR* could still be seen. Many believed that these letters **referred** to the *Mayflower* and to Harwich, the ship's home port.

Unfortunately, so few records remain that it is impossible to prove that the *Mayflower* was turned into a barn. But one thing is certain. If you look at the roof of the barn with your head tilted upside down, you can see that the hull of a ship was **definitely** used to build the roof. And that ship just may have been the *Mayflower*.

Personal Words

Choose two words from the selection that are not familiar to you or whose meanings you are not completely sure of. (Do not choose words that appear in boldfaced type.) Write the words on the lines provided. Beside each word write what you think it means, based on how it was used in the selection.

1. _____ : _____

    _____

2. _____ : _____

    _____

Using Context

A For each vocabulary word, put an **X** in the box beside its correct meaning. Try to figure out what the word means by the way it is used in the selection.

1. **concluded**
   - ☐ a. forgot
   - ☐ b. decided
   - ☐ c. pretended

2. **probable**
   - ☐ a. likely
   - ☐ b. uncertain
   - ☐ c. amusing

3. **constructed**
   - ☐ a. built
   - ☐ b. planned
   - ☐ c. contained

4. **referred**
   - ☐ a. replied to
   - ☐ b. reported to
   - ☐ c. related to

5. **definitely**
   - ☐ a. often
   - ☐ b. certainly
   - ☐ c. not likely

B Write each word from the list below beside its meaning. To figure out what each word means, go back to the passage and read the sentence that contains the word. If you can't discover the meaning from the way the word is used in the sentence, look for clues in the sentences that come before and after it.

concluded	probable	constructed	referred	definitely

1. _____ likely to occur

2. _____ put together

3. _____ surely

4. _____ associated with

5. _____ determined

Making Connections

A On the line next to each word or phrase, write the vocabulary word that is related to it. The related word or phrase may be a synonym, an antonym, or a definition for the vocabulary word.

concluded	probable	constructed	referred	definitely

1. certainly _____
2. related to _____
3. reached a decision about _____
4. fit together _____
5. unlikely _____

6. surely _____
7. took apart _____
8. came to an opinion about _____
9. likely _____
10. destroyed _____

B Complete each sentence with the correct vocabulary word.

concluded	probable	constructed	referred	definitely

1. An Inuit igloo, or hut, is _____ of blocks of hard snow.

2. Mrs. Abbot will _____ be the new principal of our school next year.

3. Travel delays are _____ because of the snowstorm.

4. The notice about soccer practice _____ only to the boy's team.

5. From the disappointed look on Colby's face, we _____ that he didn't make the team.

Personal Words Follow-up

Use a dictionary to find the definitions for the personal words you chose at the beginning of this lesson. If a word has more than one meaning, look for the meaning that defines the word as it is used in the selection. Then write the words and their dictionary definitions in the Personal Words pages at the back of the book. How close did you come to figuring out their meanings by yourself?

You have learned that when you come to a word you don't know, the context will often give you clues to its meaning. Sometimes the word itself may give you clues. Many words are made up of a root word with a prefix added to it. A prefix is a word part added at the beginning of a root word to form a new word. Prefixes have meanings, just as words do. Some prefixes even have more than one meaning. Study the table below. It shows some examples of new words formed by adding prefixes at the beginnings of root words.

Prefix	Root Word	Meaning of Prefix	New Word
dis-	+ honest	not	= dishonest
dis-	+ prove	opposite of	= disprove
mis-	+ treat	bad (ly); wrong (ly)	= mistreat
fore-	+ leg	in front	= foreleg
fore-	+ tell	before in time	= foretell
over-	+ head	above; higher	= overhead
over-	+ heat	too much; extra	= overheat
under-	+ ground	below; beneath	= underground
under-	+ cook	too little; not enough	= undercook

Notice that the word *dishonest* was formed by adding the prefix *dis-* at the beginning of the root word *honest*. What meanings does the prefix *dis-* have? You can see that the meaning of the root word *honest* combines with a meaning of the prefix *dis-* to give the meaning of the new word *dishonest*—"not honest."

Finding Meanings

Complete each sentence by using a word from the New Word column in the table above. Be sure the word makes sense in the sentence.

1. Nobody can _____ the score of the game before it is played.

2. Lower the flame on the stove or you'll _____ the soup.

3. People should not be allowed to _____ their pets.

4. The horse has been limping since it hurt its right _____.

5. Someone once had to _____ the idea that the Earth was flat.

Sense and Meaning

The boldfaced word in each sentence below is a root word with a prefix added to it. Use the context and the meanings of the root word and the prefix to figure out the correct meaning of the word. Put an **X** in the box beside the correct meaning.

1. The fireman had to **disconnect** the hose from the truck.
   - ☐ a. connect again
   - ☐ b. not connect
   - ☐ c. opposite of *connect*

2. You could see that the stray cat was weak from being **underfed**.
   - ☐ a. fed too little
   - ☐ b. fed too much
   - ☐ c. fed below

3. We could easily get lost if we **misread** the trail map.
   - ☐ a. opposite of *read*
   - ☐ b. read again
   - ☐ c. read wrongly

4. We could not **foresee** how difficult the trip across the desert would be.
   - ☐ a. know in front
   - ☐ b. know ahead of time
   - ☐ c. know wrongly

5. If you **oversleep**, you could be late for school.
   - ☐ a. sleep above
   - ☐ b. sleep too long
   - ☐ c. not sleep enough

Making Connections

The words listed below are vocabulary words you studied in this lesson. Complete each sentence with the correct word. If you need help, check back with the table at the beginning of this lesson.

| overheat | mistreat | dishonest | undercook |
| foreleg | disprove | overhead | underground |

1. It would be _____ to cheat on a test.

2. The full moon _____ was a beautiful sight.

3. Whenever Rex, our pet dog, finds a bone, he buries it _____.

4. Which _____ did the horse break when it fell?

5. If you _____ a frozen dinner, it may not be warm enough to eat.

11 | Take Me Out to the Ball Game

When you go to a professional baseball game, you can't be sure your favorite team will win. But one thing is almost **assured**. During the seventh-inning stretch, you and the rest of the fans will be standing and singing "Take Me Out to the Ball Game."

When Jack Norworth **composed** the words to his "ball song" in May 1908, he was a 30-year-old vaudeville star in New York City. He had never **witnessed** a baseball game in his life. But he wanted to come up with a fun little tune for his act, something catchy that the audience could sing along with him.

One afternoon in a subway car on his way to the theater, Norworth saw an ad from the New York Giants. The message read: "Come to the Polo Grounds and enjoy a ball game." That ad clicked with Norworth.

"I figured there had never been a baseball song," he said, "so I pulled an old hunk of paper out of my pocket and started scribbling. . . . Thirty minutes later, I had it."

When he reached the theater, Norworth **consulted** with his partner, Albert von Tilzer. Tilzer set the words to music nearly as fast as Norworth had written them. Norworth performed the song that night during his act, and the audience loved it. It wasn't long before people were singing it on street corners and at ballparks too.

Thirty-four years later, in 1942, a friend finally **persuaded** Norworth to see the Brooklyn Dodgers and the New York Giants play at Ebbets Field. After that, Norworth was hooked. "I caught the fever," he said. For the rest of his life, he was a baseball fan.

Norworth's scrap of paper, by the way, is now in the Baseball Hall of Fame in Cooperstown, New York. Not bad for an entertainer who just wanted to write a catchy little tune.

Personal Words

Choose two words from the selection that are not familiar to you or whose meanings you are not completely sure of. (Do not choose words that appear in boldfaced type.) Write the words on the lines provided. Beside each word write what you think it means, based on how it was used in the selection.

1. _____ : _____

_____

2. _____ : _____

_____

Using Context

A Put an **x** in the box beside the correct meaning for each boldfaced word. For clues to the meanings of the words, reread the parts of the passage in which they appear.

1. To say that "one thing is almost **assured**" means that one thing is almost
   - ☐ a. accepted.
   - ☐ b. certain.
   - ☐ c. forgotten.

2. When Jack Norworth **composed** the words to his "ball song," he
   - ☐ a. made up the words.
   - ☐ b. borrowed the words.
   - ☐ c. sang the words.

3. Norworth had never **witnessed** a baseball game. This means he had never
   - ☐ a. given evidence of a game.
   - ☐ b. been present to see a game.
   - ☐ c. played in a game.

4. "Norworth **consulted** with his partner" means that Norworth
   - ☐ a. asked for his partner's help or advice.
   - ☐ b. had an argument with his partner.
   - ☐ c. made friends with his partner.

5. The sentence in which *persuaded* appears helps you understand that in this context **persuaded** means
   - ☐ a. made to dislike something.
   - ☐ b. made to refuse something.
   - ☐ c. made willing to do something.

B Write each word from the list below beside its meaning. To figure out what each word means, go back to the passage and read the sentence that contains the word. If you can't discover the meaning from the way the word is used in the sentence, look for clues in the sentences that come before and after it.

assured	composed	witnessed	consulted	persuaded

1. _____ was present to see

2. _____ urged someone to do something

3. _____ asked advice from

4. _____ created a written work

5. _____ made certain

Making Connections

A On the line beside each sentence, write the vocabulary word
that has the same meaning as the underlined word or words.

assured   **composed**   **witnessed**   **consulted**   **persuaded**

1. _____ At Elena's urging, Sonia was <u>made willing</u> to run for
class president.

2. _____ Kevin <u>wrote</u> a beautiful letter to his mother for her
birthday.

3. _____ I was <u>made to feel certain</u> that I would get the job.

4. _____ Audrey <u>was there to see</u> the Rose Bowl Parade.

5. _____ Before deciding on which school to attend, Pedro
<u>looked for advice from</u> his dad.

B Complete each sentence with the correct vocabulary word.

assured   **composed**   **witnessed**   **consulted**   **persuaded**

1. Felicia had never _____ a more beautiful rainbow before.

2. Bob didn't want to go to the movies, but Homer _____
him to go.

3. Hideo's home run _____ our team's victory.

4. Angela _____ with her teacher before choosing a subject for
her report.

5. No one knows who _____ the words to our school song.

Personal Words Follow-up

Use a dictionary to find the definitions for the personal words
you chose at the beginning of this lesson. If a word has more
than one meaning, look for the meaning that defines the word
as it is used in the selection. Then write the words and their
dictionary definitions in the Personal Words pages at the back
of the book. How close did you come to figuring out their
meanings by yourself?

12 | Word Study: Suffixes

You learned that a prefix can be added at the beginning of a root word to form a new word. By knowing the meanings of the prefix and the root word, you can usually figure out the meaning of the whole word. A suffix is another word part that can help you figure out the meanings of some new words. A suffix is added to the end of a root word to form a new word. There are many suffixes that add meaning to words. For some examples, study the table below.

Root Word	Suffix	Meaning of Suffix	New Word
hope	+ -less	without; having no	= hopeless
wash	+ -able	able to be	= washable
pain	+ -ful	full of; having	= painful
fame	+ -ous	full of; having	= famous
fool	+ -ish	somewhat like	= foolish

Notice that the word *hopeless* was formed by adding the suffix *-less* to the end of the word *hope*. What meaning does the suffix *-less* have? The meaning of the root word *hope* combines with the meaning of the suffix *-less* to give the meaning of the new word *hopeless*—"without hope" or "having no hope." Sometimes there is a spelling change when a suffix is added. Notice that the *e* in *fame* was dropped before the suffix *-ous* was added to form the new word *famous*.

Finding Meanings

Complete each sentence by using a word from the New Word column in the table above. Be sure the word makes sense in the sentence.

1. If your shirt is _____, I can get that stain out.

2. It was _____ to try to burn the leaves on such a windy day.

3. Holly's sunburn seem to be more _____ at night.

4. San Francisco is one of the most _____ cities in the world.

5. I felt _____ about ever again seeing the ring I lost on the beach.

Sense and Meaning

Complete each of the following sentences by defining the
boldfaced word. If you need help, check with the table at the
beginning of the lesson.

1. Behavior that is **childish** is behavior that is _____.

2. A **dangerous** journey is a journey that is _____.

3. If a broken chair is **fixable**, it is _____.

4. A **cloudless** sky is a sky that is _____.

5. If someone is **fearful**, he or she is _____.

6. A sick person who is **curable** is _____.

7. A **yellowish** color is a color that is _____.

8. If a story is **believable**, it's a story that is _____.

9. A person who had a **sleepless** night had a night _____.

10. If a joke is **humorous**, it's a joke that is _____.

Making Connections

The words listed below are vocabulary words you studied in this
lesson. Complete each sentence with the correct word. If you
need help, check with the table at the beginning of the lesson.

famous	washable	hopeless	painful	foolish

1. Getting stung by a bee can be a _____ experience.

2. Please put those dirty trousers with the _____ clothes.

3. Andy looked _____ in that clown costume.

4. Mira dreamed of someday becoming a _____ movie star.

5. Behind by a score of 20–0, the team felt _____ about its chances
   of winning the game.

9-12 | Review and Extension

Finding Meanings

A The boldfaced words listed below are vocabulary words you studied in lessons 9 and 11. Match each word with its meaning by writing the letter of the meaning beside each word.

_____ 1. **composed**   a. decided; came to believe

_____ 2. **probable**   b. was present to see

_____ 3. **definitely**   c. put together; built

_____ 4. **persuaded**   d. made certain

_____ 5. **concluded**   e. likely to occur

_____ 6. **witnessed**   f. asked advice from

_____ 7. **referred**   g. urged someone to do something

_____ 8. **consulted**   h. certainly; surely

_____ 9. **assured**   i. related to; made a connection with

_____10. **constructed**   j. created a written work

B The boldfaced words listed below are words you studied in lesson 10. Complete each sentence with the correct word. Use what you learned about prefixes in that lesson to help you.

dishonest   **mistreat**   **overhead**   **disprove**   **foretell**

1. The hawk circled high _____ before spotting a tall tree to rest in.

2. Without any facts to support her argument, Lupe could not

   _____ the truth of Antonio's statement.

3. Some people claim they can _____ what will happen in the future.

4. A good friend would never _____ another friend.

5. People who are _____ cannot be trusted.

Sense and Meaning

The boldfaced words listed below are words you studied in
lessons 10 and 12. Beside each word, write its root word and the
prefix or suffix that has been added to it. Then write the word
in a sentence of your own on the line provided. Be sure that
the word makes sense in the sentence.

	Prefix	**Root Word**	**Suffix**
1. **washable**	_____	_____	_____
	_____		
2. **overheat**	_____	_____	_____
	_____		
3. **foolish**	_____	_____	_____
	_____		
4. **disprove**	_____	_____	_____
	_____		
5. **underground**	_____	_____	_____
	_____		
6. **famous**	_____	_____	_____
	_____		
7. **mistreat**	_____	_____	_____
	_____		
8. **hopeless**	_____	_____	_____
	_____		
9. **painful**	_____	_____	_____
	_____		
10. **foreleg**	_____	_____	_____
	_____		

Synonym Study

Following are synonym studies for two vocabulary words you studied in lessons 9 and 11. Use either the vocabulary words or their synonyms to complete the sentences in this exercise. Refer to the synonym studies as you decide which choice best fits the context of each sentence.

conclude   **decide**   **determine**

The words *conclude, decide,* and *determine* all mean "to make or cause to make a judgment about something." *Conclude* is used when a person has made a judgment about something only after carefully considering the given facts. *After studying two highway maps, Dad concluded that Route 95 is the best route to take. Decide* suggests making a judgment after considering something for a period of time. *Lori finally decided to buy the red sweater. Determine* means to make a definite and firm judgment about something. *School officials determined that the schools would be closed because of the snowstorm.*

1. Dad _____ that I was too young to start learning to drive.

2. From the evidence, the scientists _____ that wild horses once lived on the island.

3. Brad _____ to go to a movie instead of to the beach.

persuade   **convince**

Both *persuade* and *convince* mean to cause someone to believe or to do something. *Persuade* suggests getting someone to do or to believe something by appealing to his or her feelings. *Mom and I persuaded Dad to let us bring home a new puppy. Convince* means to show the truth of something with the help of sound arguments and proof. *Kosumo was able to convince Mary that he had won first prize by showing her his blue ribbon.*

4. Rosa's friends tried to _____ her to join the school band.

5. Randy's poor test score _____ him that he had to study more.

Word Forms

The boldfaced words listed below are other forms of the
vocabulary words you studied in lessons 9 and 11. Complete
each sentence with the correct word. If you are unsure of the
meaning of a word, look it up in the glossary.

construction	**probably**	**composition**	**assuring**
persuading	**definite**	**reference**	**conclusion**

1. The principal wanted a _____ answer to her question.

2. The television news story contained a _____ to our town.

3. The _____ of the new town library will begin on Monday.

4. The _____ Gail wrote for her English class is the best she's ever written.

5. After watching him make three errors in one inning, the coach reached the

   _____ that Dhann could not play third base.

6. The school library has a _____ need for more books about arts and crafts.

7. The salesperson had an easy time _____ my parents to buy a new stove.

8. If Trina feels better, she'll _____ go to the movies with us.

9. The fire chief was busy _____ everyone that the forest fire was not a threat to the town.

10. The weather will _____ turn cooler after the thunderstorm passes through.

Using Your Vocabulary

Listed below under ACROSS and DOWN are numbered
definitions of 10 vocabulary words from lessons 9 and 11.
Fill in the squares in the crossword puzzle by spelling out
the vocabulary words that fit the definitions.

ACROSS
1. built or put together
4. made something certain
6. was present to see something
8. created a written work
9. related to or associated with

DOWN
1. asked advice from
2. very likely to occur
3. urged someone to do something
5. in a certain or sure way
7. decided after carefully considering

13 | The Loch Ness Monster

The monster said to be living in the waters of Loch Ness in Scotland is not very scary. Nessie, as she is known, does not attack people. She does not destroy property. She does not try to frighten anyone. In fact, she is quite shy. Usually she goes about her own business and avoids humans. Even so, the legend of the Loch Ness monster has become one of the most **enduring** legends of our time.

Since 1933, about nine thousand sightings have been reported. Nessie has been seen both on land and in the water. Sometimes she appears when the area is almost deserted. At other times she surfaces in full view of many witnesses. Once she showed herself when a bus carrying 27 passengers was passing by. All the people aboard the bus reported that they watched the monster swim for some time.

Many people have tried to photograph Nessie. The most famous picture taken of her shows a creature of **monstrous** size, with a long, thick neck shaped somewhat like an elephant's trunk. Her head is small and flat on top, like the head of a snake. And her huge barrel-shaped body sports a 25-foot tail.

Scientists have tried to find proof of Nessie's **existence**. They looked for her with sonar, a device that is used to locate underwater objects. Some scientists believe that the sonar shows that a very large animal is indeed living in Loch Ness. Many believe that the **alleged** monsters in the photographs are simply overgrown seals or otters. Others claim that the objects seen in the water are merely sticks or logs. Part of the trouble lies with Loch Ness itself. The lake is very large. Some sections are very deep, and the water is dark and murky.

Whether or not a monster does live in the lake, just the thought that it might be there has raised many people's interest. Thousands of tourists journey to Scotland each year to **investigate** the legend of the Loch Ness monster.

Personal Words

Choose two words from the selection that are not familiar to you or whose meanings you are not completely sure of. (Do not choose words that appear in boldfaced type.) Write the words on the lines provided. Beside each word write what you think it means, based on how it was used in the selection.

1. _____ : _____

_____

2. _____ : _____

_____

Using Context

A Put an **X** in the box beside the correct meaning for each boldfaced word. For clues to the meanings of the words, reread the parts of the passage in which they appear.

1. The legend of the Loch Ness monster is one of the most **enduring** legends of our time.
   - ☐ a. believable
   - ☐ b. foolish
   - ☐ c. lasting

2. Photographs show that Nessie is a creature of **monstrous** size.
   - ☐ a. unusually large
   - ☐ b. famous
   - ☐ c. somewhat large

3. Scientists have tried to find proof of Nessie's **existence**.
   - ☐ a. being discovered
   - ☐ b. being real
   - ☐ c. being caught

4. Many people believe that the **alleged** monsters are overgrown seals.
   - ☐ a. proved true
   - ☐ b. not proved
   - ☐ c. actually stated

5. Tourists journey to Scotland to **investigate** the legend of the Loch Ness monster.
   - ☐ a. not believe
   - ☐ b. read about
   - ☐ c. look into carefully

B Read each statement below. If the statement is true, write T on the line beside the statement. If the statement is false, write F on the line.

_____ 1. If you investigate something, you examine it thoroughly.

_____ 2. If an event is alleged to have taken place, it is certain that it did take place.

_____ 3. To describe something as being monstrous means that it is small but scary.

_____ 4. *Black Beauty* is an enduring favorite of generations of children.

_____ 5. If you doubt the existence of something, you are not sure that it is real.

50

Making Connections

A On the line beside each word or phrase, write the vocabulary word that is related to it. The related word or phrase may be a synonym, an antonym, or a definition.

enduring	monstrous	existence	alleged	investigate

1. supposed   _____

2. brief   _____

3. to examine closely _____

4. continuing   _____

5. certain   _____

6. small   _____

7. being real   _____

8. huge   _____

9. lasting   _____

10. to ignore   _____

B Complete each sentence with the correct vocabulary word.

enduring	monstrous	existence	alleged	investigate

1. Saber-toothed tigers are no longer in _____.

2. *Enormous* is a good synonym for _____.

3. The two men had an _____ friendship that lasted for 50 years.

4. It has been _____ that the stranger stole Ken's watch.

5. The police will _____ the theft of the watch.

Personal Words Follow-up

Use a dictionary to find the definitions for the personal words you chose at the beginning of this lesson. If a word has more than one meaning, look for the meaning that defines the word as it is used in the selection. Then write the words and their dictionary definitions in the Personal Words pages.

14 | Word Study: Analogies

Sometimes things that seem quite different can be similar or related to each other in one or more ways. For example, a bird and an airplane are quite different, yet they are related to each other in two important ways. Both have wings, and both can fly. We say that there is an analogy between a bird and an airplane. An analogy is defined as "a likeness in certain ways between things that are otherwise unlike."

A pen and an author are related in one particular way. A pen is a tool that an author uses for writing. A similar relationship exists between a brush and an artist. A brush is a tool that an artist uses for painting. The relationship between the two word pairs *pen* and *author* and *brush* and *artist* is so similar that we can state them both in a sentence like this:

Pen is to **author** as **brush** is to **artist**.

This sentence states an analogy between the word pair *pen* and *author* and the word pair *brush* and *artist*. Read the following analogy.

Rose is to **flower** as **carrot** is to **vegetable**.

Can you figure out the relationship between the two word pairs? Yes, a rose is a kind of flower as a carrot is a kind of vegetable.

The following analogy is not complete. To complete it, first determine the relationship between the words in the first word pair. Then choose a word that will show a similar relationship between the two words in the second pair.

Short is to **tall** as **weak** is to _____.

Did you choose *strong*? *Strong* is the opposite of *weak*, just as *tall* is the opposite of *short*.

Finding Meanings

Circle the word that correctly completes each analogy.

1. **Head** is to **hat** as **hand** is to _____.	finger	sock	glove
2. **Train** is to **track** as **car** is to _____.	garage	road	bridge
3. **Teacher** is to **school** as **doctor** is to _____.	medicine	hospital	nurse
4. **Monday** is to **week** as **July** is to _____.	year	summer	day
5. **Bee** is to **hive** as **bird** is to _____.	nest	seed	wings

Sense and Meaning

Use a word from the list below to complete each of the following analogies.

green	cage	sweet	garage	baseball
sad	bird	pencil	ears	kitten

1. **Horse** is to **stable** as **car** is to _____.

2. **Sight** is to **eyes** as **sound** is to _____.

3. **Ink** is to **pen** as **lead** is to _____.

4. **Racket** is to **tennis** as **bat** is to _____.

5. **Sky** is to **blue** as **grass** is to _____.

6. **Dog** is to **puppy** as **cat** is to _____.

7. **Mouth** is to **person** as **beak** is to _____.

8. **Easy** is to **hard** as **happy** is to _____.

9. **Fish** is to **tank** as **bird** is to _____.

10. **Lemon** is to **sour** as **sugar** is to _____.

Making Connections

Write the word that correctly completes each analogy.

1. **Carpenter** is to **hammer** as _____ is to **plow**.

    farmer   horse   garden

2. **Cool** is to **cold** as _____ is to **hot**.

    sun   fire   warm

3. **Trout** is to **fish** as _____ is to **insect**.

    robin   turtle   ant

4. **Toes** are to **feet** as _____ are to **hands**.

    elbow   fingers   thumbs

5. **Up** is to **down** as _____ is to **bottom**.

    top   under   over

15 | Disasters at Sea

The year was 1912. The *Titanic* was on its first trip, sailing from Southampton, England, to New York City. Newspapers called the *Titanic* "a seagoing hotel" and "the safest ship afloat." The captain wanted to prove that the *Titanic* was also the fastest ship. For that reason, he kept the *Titanic* moving at a fast pace for most of the voyage.

In mid-April, the Atlantic waters are icy cold. Two nearby ships sent warning messages to the *Titanic*. The ships **revealed** that they had seen many icebergs, large masses of ice. In spite of the warnings, the *Titanic* continued rapidly on its way.

Suddenly a huge iceberg loomed in the *Titanic*'s path. The first officer ordered the ship to turn. Then he signaled the engine room to stop. The *Titanic* turned to one side, as if in slow motion. Too late! With a long, grinding sound, the *Titanic* scraped along the side of the iceberg. The passengers heard the sound but felt no sense of danger. They believed that the ship's thick hull was **sufficient** to resist any harm. In the engine room, the crew tried to **maintain** control of the ship. They could see that the damage was serious. The iceberg had ripped a long, jagged gash into the ship below the waterline. The sea was pouring in.

The *Titanic* was going down. The captain gave the order for everyone to leave the ship. But there were enough lifeboats for only half of the 2,200 people on board. Two hours later, the ship sank. In the confusion, only 711 passengers were saved.

Another **disaster** involving a ship at sea occurred on March 24, 1989. This time no human lives were lost. Great damage was caused to animals and the environment, however. The oil tanker *Exxon Valdez* ran aground on Bligh Reef off the coast of Alaska. More than 11 million gallons of oil were spilled into the sea. The oil killed more than 30,000 seabirds and **polluted** an area of 500 square miles.

Personal Words

Choose two words from the selection that are not familiar to you or whose meanings you are not completely sure of. (Do not choose words that appear in boldfaced type.) Write the words on the lines provided. Beside each word write what you think it means, based on how it was used in the selection.

1. _____ : _____

_____

2. _____ : _____

_____

Using Context

A For each vocabulary word, put an **X** in the box beside its correct meaning. Try to figure out what the word means by the way it is used in the selection.

1. **revealed**
   - ☐ a. covered up
   - ☐ b. made known
   - ☐ c. repeated

2. **sufficient**
   - ☐ a. several
   - ☐ b. enough
   - ☐ c. shortage of

3. **maintain**
   - ☐ a. bring to an end
   - ☐ b. delay
   - ☐ c. carry on

4. **disaster**
   - ☐ a. great misfortune
   - ☐ b. important event
   - ☐ c. violent storm

5. **polluted**
   - ☐ a. made dirty
   - ☐ b. made clean
   - ☐ c. made safe

B Each of the following questions can be answered with yes or no. If your answer to a question is yes, write Y on the line before the question. If your answer is no, write N on the line.

_____ 1. Would it be all right to swim in a **polluted** pond?

_____ 2. If you **revealed** a secret to friends, would you be letting them know what the secret is?

_____ 3. If a strong earthquake were to strike a large city, would it likely cause a **disaster**?

_____ 4. If you **maintain** a friendship with someone, does it mean that you've just started that friendship?

_____ 5. Would a town with a **sufficient** water supply need to find more water?

Making Connections

A Use one of the vocabulary words below to correctly complete each of the following analogies. Remember that in an analogy, the words in the second word pair must be related to each other in the same way that the words in the first word pair are related.

    revealed   **sufficient**   **maintain**   **disaster**   **polluted**

1. **Happiness** is to **joy** as **tragedy** is to _____.

2. **Separate** is to **join** as **stop** is to _____.

3. **Huge** is to **enormous** as **enough** is to _____.

4. **Created** is to **destroyed** as **cleaned** is to _____.

5. **Found** is to **discovered** as **showed** is to _____.

B Listed below are some synonyms and antonyms for five vocabulary words from this lesson. Next to each vocabulary word, write its synonym and antonym.

spoiled   enough   cleaned   tragedy   insufficient

continue   stop   hid   showed   success

	Synonym	**Antonym**
1. **revealed**	_____	_____
2. **sufficient**	_____	_____
3. **maintain**	_____	_____
4. **disaster**	_____	_____
5. **polluted**	_____	_____

Personal Words Follow-up

Use a dictionary to find the definitions for the personal words you chose at the beginning of this lesson. If a word has more than one meaning, look for the meaning that defines the word as it is used in the selection. Then write the words and their dictionary definitions in the Personal Words pages.

16 | Word Study: Idioms

Idioms are words or phrases that have meanings quite different from the literal or usual meanings of the words themselves. For example, note the boldfaced words in these two sentences:

1. During the storm, a tall pine tree was blown over and **hit the roof** of our house.
2. When Dad saw Kevin's poor grades on his report card, he **hit the roof**.

Do you think the phrase *hit the roof* has the same meaning in each of these sentences? In sentence 1, these words are used with their usual meaning. They mean that the falling pine tree actually hit the roof of the house. In sentence 2, do you think Dad actually *hit the roof* when he saw Kevin's poor report card? No, that wouldn't make any sense. In that sentence, the phrase *hit the roof* is used with a special meaning. It means that Kevin's dad was angry or upset about Kevin's poor grades.

In sentence 2 the phrase *hit the roof* is an *idiom*. If you come across a word or phrase that doesn't seem to mean what it usually does, it may be an idiom. If you don't know the special meaning the idiom has, use the context to help you figure out a meaning that makes sense.

Finding Meanings

Two possible meanings are given for the underlined idiom in each sentence. On the line next to the sentence, write the letter of the correct meaning. Use the context to help you.

_____ 1. Pei-ying thought all wealthy people had <u>money to burn</u>.

        a. money to set on fire   b. extra money to spend

_____ 2. Marty told his annoying sister to <u>go fly a kite</u>.

        a. send a kite into the air   b. go away

_____ 3. At the chess club meeting, Alicia asked if she could <u>take the floor</u>.

        a. stand up to talk   b. pick up the floor

_____ 4. Mom <u>put her foot down</u> when Antoine asked her if he could stay out late.

        a. tapped her foot on the floor   b. firmly refused

Sense and Meaning

Use the context to help you figure out the meaning of the underlined idiom in each sentence below. Then put an **X** in the box beside the answer that gives the correct meaning of the sentence.

1. Jan thought that Ida should plan the cake sale. "That's her <u>cup of tea</u>," she said.
   - ☐ a. Jan thought Ida should serve tea at the cake sale.
   - ☐ b. Jan pointed out that the cup of tea was Ida's.
   - ☐ c. Jan thought planning a cake sale would be the kind of thing Ida would like to do.

2. Ana and James didn't agree about many things, but they <u>saw eye to eye</u> about what to get their dad for his birthday.
   - ☐ a. Ana and James disagreed about what to get their dad.
   - ☐ b. Ana and James saw the same present with their own eyes.
   - ☐ c. Ana and Jim agreed completely about what to get their dad.

3. Jeff couldn't help us because he <u>had his hands full</u> painting the fence.
   - ☐ a. Jeff was too busy painting the fence to help.
   - ☐ b. Jeff's hands were too full of paint to help.
   - ☐ c. Jeff's hands were too full carrying the paint and brush.

4. Lilla said she would <u>jump at the chance</u> to be the team captain.
   - ☐ a. Lilla would jump with joy if she became the team captain.
   - ☐ b. Lilla would eagerly accept the chance to be the team captain.
   - ☐ c. Lilla would be too jumpy, or nervous, to be the team captain.

Making Connections

An idiom is underlined in each sentence below. Match each idiom with its meaning. Write the letter of its meaning on the line next to the sentence.

_____ 1. The party will be a big surprise to Wanda if no one <u>spills the beans</u>.

_____ 2. Dad <u>weighed the matter</u> before deciding to buy a new computer.

_____ 3. I asked Miguel and Joe, but they wouldn't <u>lift a finger</u> to help me.

_____ 4. Will didn't have much money, but he was able to buy a used catcher's mitt <u>for a song</u>.

a. weighed the computer	e. raise their hands
b. very cheaply	f. tips over a pot of beans
c. by trading a song for it	g. do the slightest thing
d. reveals a secret too soon	h. thought carefully about

13-16 | Review and Extension

Finding Meanings

A The boldfaced words listed below are vocabulary words you studied in lessons 13 and 15. Match each word with its meaning by writing the letter of its meaning beside each word.

_____ 1. **existence**   a. to look into carefully; to examine closely

_____ 2. **revealed**   b. made dirty; spoiled

_____ 3. **investigate**   c. lasting

_____ 4. **maintain**   d. made known; showed

_____ 5. **enduring**   e. stated without proof; supposed

_____ 6. **polluted**   f. unusually large; huge; enormous

_____ 7. **alleged**   g. enough

_____ 8. **sufficient**   h. state of being

_____ 9. **monstrous**   i. to carry on; to continue

_____ 10. **disaster**   j. great misfortune

B The boldfaced words listed below are words you studied in lesson 13. Use one of those words to correctly complete each of the following analogies. Remember that in an analogy, the words in the second word pair must be related to each other in the same way that the words in the first word pair are related.

enduring   **monstrous**   **existence**   **alleged**   **investigate**

1. **Sure** is to **certain** as **doubtful** is to _____.

2. **Hide** is to **reveal** as **ignore** is to _____.

3. **Last** is to **final** as **lasting** is to _____.

4. **Wise** is to **foolish** as **small** is to _____.

5. **Beginning** is to **start** as **life** is to _____.

Sense and Meaning

Remember that an idiom is a word or phrase that means
something different from the meaning the words usually have.
An idiom that you studied in lesson 16 is underlined in each of
the following sentences. Rewrite each sentence, stating in your
own words what the idiom really means.

1. From his unhappy look, I could tell that dancing was not Lee's <u>cup of tea</u>.

   _____

2. "Unless you have <u>money to burn</u>, don't buy that dress," said Mom.

   _____

3. "I'd <u>jump at the chance</u> to go to the Cubs game today," said Louis.

   _____

4. Maura can't help us because she <u>has her hands full</u> baby-sitting.

   _____

5. When I broke Lenny's favorite bat, he <u>hit the roof</u>.

   _____

6. Meg <u>weighed the matter</u> of which college to attend for a long time.

   _____

7. The judges all <u>saw eye to eye</u> with each other.

   _____

8. When I asked Chanuba to trade magazines, she told me to <u>go fly a kite</u>.

   _____

9. Salvatore wanted a new bike, but he knew he could not buy one <u>for a song</u>.

   _____

10. Liz <u>put her foot down</u> when her sister asked to borrow her new jacket.

   _____

Synonym Study

Following are synonym studies for two vocabulary words you studied in lessons 13 and 15. Use either the vocabulary words or their synonyms to complete the sentences in this exercise. Check with the synonym studies as you decide which choice best fits the context of each sentence.

enduring   **lasting**   **permanent**

The words *enduring, lasting,* and *permanent* all mean "continuing for a long period of time or forever." *Enduring* suggests the idea of continuing despite the passage of a long period of time. *Sarah had an enduring memory of her great grandfather. Lasting* suggests something going on for a period of time longer than would normally be expected. *Striking out in his last at-bat of the season is still a lasting memory for Shane. Permanent* suggests something that is not likely to end or change for a long time or, perhaps, never. *A statue was placed in the park as a permanent memorial to the town's war heroes.*

1. Losing the talent contest to her younger sister had a _____ effect on Sasheen.

2. After working part time at the bank for six months, Keisha was given a

   _____ position.

3. *The Wizard of Oz* is one of the most _____ movies of all time.

sufficient   **enough**

Sufficient and *enough* both have to do with meeting some kind of need. *Sufficient* suggests that a need has been nearly or closely met, neither much under or much over what is needed. *There has been a sufficient amount of rainfall to grow a good crop this year.* The word *enough* suggests that whatever is needed is present but not in *an amount that is greater than needed. *There is enough water on the ship for the voyage.*

4. Bruce said he had just _____ money to buy a ticket to the movie.

5. The teacher said we had a _____ number of books for the class.

Word Forms

The boldfaced words listed below are other forms of the vocabulary words you studied in lessons 13 and 15. Fill in the blank in each sentence with the proper word. If you are unsure of the meaning of a word, look it up in the glossary.

pollution	**endure**	**disastrous**	**investigation**
allege	**exist**	**revealing**	**sufficiently**

1. When the passenger ship *Titanic* hit an iceberg, the result was

   _____.

2. The judges will be _____ the names of the contest winners on Friday.

3. Air _____ is a serious health concern in many American cities.

4. It is a known fact that human beings cannot _____ without water.

5. The Pilgrims who sailed to America on the *Mayflower* had to _____ many hardships during the long voyage.

6. The climbers were _____ supplied with food and water before they began their long climb to the top of the mountain.

7. The thick clouds blew away, _____ a beautiful rainbow in the sky.

8. The fire department will start an _____ to find out what caused the fire.

9. There are still many people who _____ that a monster really lives in the deep waters of Loch Ness.

10. There are many more people, however, who insist that the Loch Ness monster does

    not _____ at all.

62

Using Your Vocabulary

The scrambled words in boldface below are vocabulary words you studied in lessons 13 and 15. Rearrange the letters of each word to form its correct spelling. Then use the word to complete the sentence next to it. Be sure the word makes sense in the sentence. If you need to, look back at the vocabulary words in lessons 13 and 15.

1. **natminia**

1. Our class will _____ the tradition of planting flowers in front of the school.

2. **ledlaeg**

2. Even though she didn't see him, Mrs. Adleman _____ that Ben broke her window.

3. **uiftcisnef**

3. The florist told me to make sure that this plant receives a _____ amount of sunlight.

4. **ortsnumso**

4. The redwood trees in California are not just very large, they are _____.

5. **dlupelot**

5. The beach had to be closed to swimmers because the water was _____.

6. **gedrninu**

6. There is an _____ spirit of freedom in the United States.

7. **evdaerel**

7. Everyone was surprised when it was _____ that our principal is going to retire.

8. **igetintaves**

8. Jaque was afraid to _____ the strange noises he heard coming from the attic.

9. **redsitas**

9. It was a terrible _____ when the dam burst and flooded the valley below.

10. **centxeise**

10. Scientists question the _____ of life on other planets.

17 | Glaciers on the Move

In 1933 two park rangers were hiking across Lyell Glacier in Yosemite National Park in California. It was a warm, sunny day. The rangers were enjoying the view. As they looked around, one of the rangers was startled by what he saw. There was a mountain sheep staring right at him. The ranger knew this wasn't just any sheep. The animal he was looking at was supposed to be **extinct**.

The rangers moved slowly toward the sheep. They were amazed that it didn't run away. It stood as still as a statue. When the rangers touched the animal, they knew why it hadn't moved. It was frozen solid. The sheep had died a long, long time ago, but it had been perfectly **preserved** by the ice. Because it had a broken neck, scientists concluded that the animal had died when it had fallen into a huge crack in the glacier. The sheep had been buried below tons of ice for many years. As the glacier slowly moved and melted, the sheep's body was uncovered. The rangers who found the mountain sheep just happened to be in the right place at the right time.

Glaciers are made up of snow and ice that have **accumulated** over many years. But not every pile of snow and ice is a glacier. A pile of ice and snow can be called a glacier only if it moves under its own weight.

When fresh snow falls on top of the last year's snow, its weight presses the snowflakes underneath together to form a coarse material called firn. Year after year, more layers of snow fall on top of the firn. More snow means more weight and more pressure. The crystals deep inside the snow pile are crushed and **compacted** by the weight of the layers on top of them.

Eventually, the lower layers become much thicker than the layers close to the surface. Finally, the snow particles can't take any more pressure. So they melt and then refreeze to form ice.

Personal Words

Choose two words from the selection that are not familiar to you or whose meanings you are not completely sure of. (Do not choose words that appear in boldfaced type.) Write the words on the lines provided. Beside each word write what you think it means, based on how it was used in the selection.

1. _____ : _____

_____

2. _____ : _____

_____

Using Context

A Put an **X** in the box beside the correct meaning for each boldfaced word. For clues to the meanings of the words, reread the parts of the passage in which they appear.

1. The rangers thought that the animal was **extinct**. This means that the animal the rangers were looking at was supposed to be
   - ☐ a. up in the mountains.
   - ☐ b. afraid of them.
   - ☐ c. no longer in existence.

2. The mountain sheep had been perfectly **preserved**. This means that the sheep had been
   - ☐ a. kept from changing or rotting.
   - ☐ b. kept alive.
   - ☐ c. lost for a long time.

3. The sentence in which **accumulated** appears helps you understand that in this context *accumulated* means
   - ☐ a. piled up.
   - ☐ b. melted into water.
   - ☐ c. would not mix together.

4. The sentence in which **compacted** appears helps you understand that in this context *compacted* means
   - ☐ a. pulled apart.
   - ☐ b. packed closely together.
   - ☐ c. completely destroyed.

5. "**Eventually**, the lower layers become much thicker," means that
   - ☐ a. in the beginning, the lower layers become much thicker.
   - ☐ b. after a short time, the lower layers become much thicker.
   - ☐ c. in the end, the lower layers become much thicker.

B Write each word from the list below beside its meaning. To figure out what each word means, go back to the passage and read the sentence that contains the word. If you can't discover the meaning from the way the word is used in the sentence, look for clues in the sentences that come before and after it.

extinct	preserved	accumulated	compacted	eventually

1. _____ piled up; increased in amount

2. _____ no longer in existence

3. _____ packed closely together

4. _____ kept from changing or rotting

5. _____ in the end; finally

Making Connections

A The boldfaced words listed below are vocabulary words from this lesson. Use one of these words to complete each of the following analogies. Remember that in an analogy, the words in the second word pair must be related to each other in the same way that the words in the first word pair are related.

    extinct   **preserved**   **accumulated**   **compacted**   **eventually**

1. **Scattered** is to **gathered** as **separated** is to _____.

2. **Beginning** is to **start** as **finally** is to _____.

3. **Appeared** is to **vanished** as **living** is to _____.

4. **Save** is to **keep** as **collected** is to _____.

5. **Protected** is to **guarded** as **maintained** is to _____.

B On the line next to each word or phrase, write the vocabulary word that is related to it. The related word or phrase may be a synonym, an antonym, or a definition for the vocabulary word.

    extinct   **preserved**   **accumulated**   **compacted**   **eventually**

1. destroyed _____

2. gathered _____

3. finally _____

4. spread out _____

5. tightly packed together _____

6. separated _____

7. in the end _____

8. exists _____

9. collected _____

10. kept from rotting _____

Personal Words Follow-up

Use a dictionary to help you find the definitions for the personal words you chose at the beginning of this lesson. If a word has more than one meaning, look for the meaning that defines the word as it is used in the selection. Then write the words and their dictionary definitions in the Personal Words pages at the back of the book.

18 | Word Study: Prefixes

Remember that a prefix is a word part added at the beginning of a root word to form a new word. You have learned that prefixes have meanings just as words do. When you come to a word that looks unfamiliar to you, it could be a familiar root word with a prefix added at its beginning. Study the table below. It shows some more examples of new words formed by adding prefixes at the beginning of root words.

Prefix	Root Word	Meaning of Prefix	New Word
in-	+ expensive	not; opposite of	= inexpensive
im-	+ polite	not; opposite of	= impolite
il-	+ legal	not; opposite of	= illegal
ir-	+ regular	not; opposite of	= irregular
out-	+ live	more than; longer than	= outlive
out-	+ run	better than	= outrun

You can see that the word *inexpensive* was formed by adding the prefix *in-* at the beginning of the root word *expensive*. The prefix *in-* means "not" or "opposite of." Combining the meaning of the root word *expensive* with the meaning of the prefix *in-* gives the meaning of the new word *inexpensive*— "not expensive." Before certain letters, *in-* changes its spelling but not its meaning. You will see *im-* used before root words beginning with *b, m,* or *p.* Before *r, in-* becomes *ir-,* and before *l,* it becomes *il-.* See the table above for some examples.

Finding Meanings

Complete each sentence by using a word from the New Word column in the table above. Be sure that the word makes sense in the sentence.

1. If you receive a party invitation, it would be _____ not to reply.

2. Mr. Ames, who is 95 years old, hadn't expected to _____ his younger brother.

3. Jackie was pleased to learn how _____ theater tickets are.

4. Monty's _____ heartbeat worried his doctor.

5. It is _____ to throw trash on the ground in a public park.

66

Sense and Meaning

Each of the following questions can be answered yes or no. If your answer to a question is yes, write Y on the line before the question. If your answer is no, write N on the line.

_____ 1. Would you be able to do an **impossible** task?

_____ 2. If you **outweigh** someone, do you weigh more than that person?

_____ 3. Would a person who does something **illegal** be breaking the law?

_____ 4. If your savings were **insufficient** to pay for a new CD player, would you have enough money to buy it?

_____ 5. Would it be considered **irregular** for someone to eat his or her dessert before eating dinner?

Making Connections

The words listed below are vocabulary words you studied in this lesson. Complete each sentence with the correct word. If you need help, check back with the table at the beginning of this lesson.

illegal   **inexpensive**   **impolite**   **outrun**   **irregular**   **outlive**

1. A person who stares at another person is being _____.

2. In some places, fishing without a license is _____.

3. By beating Drew in a footrace, Chris proved she could _____ him.

4. A word that is a synonym for *cheap* is _____.

5. Sometimes when people are very sick, their breathing becomes _____.

19 A Story of Courage

In 1307 Switzerland was not a free country as it is today. It was under the rule of Austria. The freedom-loving Swiss hated the Austrians. They especially hated a man named Gessler, who was **appointed** governor of the town of Altdorf. The ruler of Austria had sent Gessler there to **represent** him.

Gessler was a cruel man. To show the people his authority, he had his cap placed on a pole and ordered that everyone should bow down before it. One man, William Tell, refused to do so. According to legend, Gessler became angry and ordered Tell to shoot an apple off his son's head. Tell was able to **accomplish** this because he was an expert with a bow and arrow. Gessler noticed that Tell had an extra arrow in his belt. He asked Tell what he had planned to do with the second arrow. "It was for you if I had hurt my son with the first arrow," Tell answered.

Gessler had his men **seize** Tell. They put him into a boat to take him to a prison across a lake. As they crossed the lake, a terrible storm came up. Tell was the **sole** person onboard who could handle the boat in such a storm, so Gessler had his chains removed. When the boat reached the shore, Tell leaped out of the boat and escaped into the woods.

Tell's great courage inspired the Swiss to fight for and eventually gain their freedom from Austria. Is his story completely true? No one really knows. We do know that William Tell lived during that time and that he is still a national hero in Switzerland.

Personal Words

Choose two words from the selection that are not familiar to you or whose meanings you are not completely sure of. (Do not choose words that appear in boldfaced type.) Write the words on the lines provided. Beside each word write what you think it means, based on how it was used in the selection.

1. _____ : _____

_____

2. _____ : _____

_____

Using Context

A Put an **X** in the box beside the correct meaning for each boldfaced word. For clues to the meanings of the words, reread the parts of the passage in which they appear.

1. They especially did not like a man named Gessler, who was **appointed** the governor of the town of Altdorf.
   - ☐ a. meeting with
   - ☐ b. selected to be
   - ☐ c. reporting to

2. The ruler of Austria had sent Gessler to Altdorf to **represent** him.
   - ☐ a. praise
   - ☐ b. act for
   - ☐ c. protect

3. Tell was able to **accomplish** this task, for he was an expert with a bow and arrow.
   - ☐ a. avoid doing
   - ☐ b. enjoy doing
   - ☐ c. succeed in doing

4. Gessler had his men **seize** Tell.
   - ☐ a. grab onto
   - ☐ b. let go of
   - ☐ c. follow

5. Tell was the **sole** person on board who could handle the boat in such a storm.
   - ☐ a. last
   - ☐ b. only
   - ☐ c. strongest

B Read each statement below. If the statement is true, write T on the line beside the statement. If the statement is false, write F on the line.

_____ 1. If you **accomplished** something you planned to do, you succeeded in doing it.

_____ 2. If you were the **sole** person in a room, you would not be alone in that room.

_____ 3. To **seize** something means to pick it up slowly and gently.

_____ 4. Two friends who ask you to **represent** them at a school meeting want you to act and speak in their places.

_____ 5. Mr. O'Brien was **appointed** the new basketball coach. This means that Mr. O'Brien was disappointed because he was not chosen to be the new coach.

Making Connections

A On the line beside each sentence, write the vocabulary word that has the same meaning as the underlined word or words.

> appointed　　　represent　　　accomplish　　　seize　　　sole

1. _____ Rita was able to <u>succeed in completing</u> all the work she had planned.

2. _____ Ben tried to <u>suddenly grab</u> my book, but I was holding it too tightly.

3. _____ Lynn hoped that she would be <u>chosen</u> to serve on the dance committee.

4. _____ Lewis was the <u>one and only</u> player to miss the team bus.

5. _____ People usually hire lawyers to <u>speak for</u> them in court.

B Complete each sentence with the correct vocabulary word.

> appointed　　　represent　　　accomplish　　　seize　　　sole

1. Wendy was convinced that she could _____ the task she was given to do.

2. Three students will _____ our school in the citywide spelling bee.

3. After the first day, Mario was the _____ student from our school left in the spelling bee.

4. Brenda was _____ by the teacher to be the classroom messenger.

5. Dad had to _____ the paddle quickly before it fell out of the boat.

Personal Words Follow-up

Use a dictionary to help you find the definitions for the personal words you chose at the beginning of this lesson. If a word has more than one meaning, look for the meaning that defines the word as it is used in the selection. Then write the words and their dictionary definitions in the Personal Words pages at the back of the book.

20 Word Study: Suffixes

Remember that a suffix is a word part added to the end of a root word to form a new word. In many cases, adding a suffix to a word changes the word's part of speech. For some more examples of suffixes and their meanings, study the table below.

Root Word	Suffix	Meaning of Suffix	New Word
bright	+ -en	to make; to cause to be	= brighten
wool	+ -en	made of	= woolen
month	+ -ly	every	= monthly
quiet	+ -ly	in a certain way	= quietly
excite	+ -ment	state or condition of being	= excitement
agree	+ -ment	product or result of	= agreement
sick	+ -ness	condition of being	= sickness
home	+ -ward	in the direction of; toward	= homeward

Notice that the suffixes -en, -ly, and -ment are each listed twice. That's because these suffixes have more than one meaning. For example, the suffix -en in the word *brighten* means "to make or cause to be." So, if you *brighten* a room, you make or cause it to be bright. The suffix -en in *woolen* means "made of." A *woolen* coat is made of wool. Knowing the meanings of suffixes can often help you figure out the meanings of unfamiliar words.

Finding Meanings

Complete each sentence by using a word from the New Word column in the table above. Be sure that the word makes sense in the sentence.

1. After discussing the problem, the two sides reached an _____.

2. We were lost, but our dog led us _____.

3. Carrie was not looking forward to her _____ visit to the dentist.

4. The bird didn't hear the cat that was _____ creeping toward it.

5. Jeremy's _____ will prevent him from going on the school field trip.

Sense and Meaning

Complete each of the following sentences by defining the
boldfaced word. If you need help, check with the table at the
beginning of the lesson.

1. A **wooden** bridge is a bridge that is _____.

2. If you look **skyward**, you would be looking _____.

3. A **weekly** magazine is one that is published _____.

4. If you **sharpen** a knife, you _____.

5. **Improvement** is the _____.

6. If you act **wisely**, you will be acting _____.

7. **Softness** is the _____.

8. A **silken** robe is a robe that is _____.

9. **Amazement** is the _____.

10. When the pioneers traveled **westward**, they were traveling _____.

Making Connections

The boldfaced words listed below are vocabulary words you
studied in this lesson. Complete each sentence with the correct
word. If you need help, check with the table at the beginning of
the lesson.

agreement	brighten	monthly	excitement
sickness	woolen	quietly	homeward

1. Alfredo couldn't hide his _____ as he watched the fireworks
   display.

2. Even though the long hike in the woods was enjoyable, we were all glad to be heading

   _____.

3. Bryant can stay in the library if he agrees to work _____.

4. Marisa and Betsy could not come to an _____ about what movie
   to see.

5. A fresh coat of white paint certainly helped to _____ Tomas's room.

17-20 Review and Extension

Finding Meanings

A The boldfaced words listed below are vocabulary words you studied in lessons 17 and 19. Match each word with its meaning by writing the letter of its meaning beside the word.

_____ 1. **accomplish**   a. kept from changing or rotting

_____ 2. **eventually**   b. to grab onto suddenly

_____ 3. **appointed**   c. in the end; finally

_____ 4. **preserved**   d. to act and speak for

_____ 5. **sole**   e. piled up; collected

_____ 6. **represent**   f. one and only

_____ 7. **extinct**   g. to succeed in doing

_____ 8. **compacted**   h. no longer in existence

_____ 9. **seize**   i. selected to be

_____10. **accumulated**   j. packed closely together

B The boldfaced words listed below are words you studied in lesson 18. Fill in the blank in each sentence with the correct word. Use what you learned about prefixes in that lesson to help you.

irregular   **outrun**   **impolite**   **inexpensive**   **outlive**   **illegal**

1. The suspect was caught because he could not _____ the police dog.

2. It is _____ to wear a hat while eating in a restaurant.

3. During a fire emergency, firefighters must work _____ hours.

4. You can find many _____ items in a bargain store.

5. In England it is _____ to drive a car on the right side of the road.

73

Sense and Meaning

The boldfaced words listed below are words you studied in
lessons 18 and 20. Beside each word, write its root word and the
prefix or suffix that has been added to it. Then write the word
in a sentence on the line provided. Be sure that the word
makes sense in the sentence.

	Prefix	Root Word	Suffix
1. **agreement**	_____	_____	_____
2. **irregular**	_____	_____	_____
3. **outrun**	_____	_____	_____
4. **brighten**	_____	_____	_____
5. **homeward**	_____	_____	_____
6. **inexpensive**	_____	_____	_____
7. **monthly**	_____	_____	_____
8. **illegal**	_____	_____	_____
9. **sickness**	_____	_____	_____
10. **impolite**	_____	_____	_____

Synonym Study

Following are synonym studies for two vocabulary words you
studied in lessons 17 and 19. Use either the vocabulary words
or their synonyms to complete the sentences in this exercise.
Refer to the synonym studies as you decide which choice best
fits the context of each sentence.

accumulate   amass

The words *accumulate* and *amass* can both mean "to collect or to gather together
some amount of something." *Accumulate* is generally used when whatever is collected
or gathered is done little by little over a long period of time. *Over his lifetime, he
accumulated a large collection of rare books.* The word *amass* suggests that whatever is
collected or gathered is done within a relatively short period of time. *She was able to
amass a huge fortune in only five years.*

1. Detectives have _____ a large amount of evidence in the past week.

2. Tessa has _____ more than 50 dolls for her collection.

accomplish   achieve

Both the word *accomplish* and the word *achieve* include the idea of carrying out some
task to a successful end. *Accomplish* stresses the result rather than the process. *What did
Eddie accomplish by quitting his job?* The word *achieve* suggests that things standing in the
way had to be overcome with great effort before a successful result could be reached.
Because of her weeks of hard work, Ella achieved the highest score in the class.

3. I can _____ more in a day than my brother can in a week.

4. Despite her blindness, Marianne was able to _____ great fame
as a singer.

Word Forms

The boldfaced words listed below are other forms of the vocabulary words you studied in lessons 17 and 19. Complete each sentence with the correct word. If you are unsure of the meaning of a word, look it up in the glossary.

appointment   **compact**   **accumulation**   **eventual**   **accomplishment**

preservative   **seizure**   **extinction**   **solely**   **representative**

1. Many people worked hard to save the bald eagle from _____.

2. Salt is considered a good _____ for meat.

3. There was a great _____ of dust under Phillipo's bed.

4. It was a long and hard-fought game, but the Owls were the _____ winners.

5. With Karen's support, Jessie's _____ to the student council was made certain.

6. Ed O'Reilly was elected to be our new _____ in the United States Congress.

7. Landing astronauts on the moon was a great _____ for this country's space program.

8. Anthony said that he was _____ responsible for the broken window.

9. Erin's teacher praised her for getting so much information into such a

   _____ report.

10. The Coast Guard will explain its _____ of the ship's cargo.

Using Your Vocabulary

Listed below under ACROSS and DOWN are numbered definitions of 10 vocabulary words from lessons 17 and 19. Fill in the squares in the crossword puzzle by spelling out the vocabulary words that fit the definitions.

ACROSS
1. piled up; collected
4. kept from changing or rotting
6. one and only
8. in the end; finally
10. selected to be

DOWN
2. packed closely together
3. grab onto suddenly
5. act and speak for
7. no longer in existence
9. succeed in doing

21 | Trudy Ederle's Swim of a Lifetime

Stroke. Stroke. Stroke. Gertrude "Trudy" Ederle was 14 miles off the coast of France and 7 miles from her goal—the coast of England. She had been swimming for 11 hours through frigid water. Rain beat down, the tide dragged her backward, and the salty water had caused her tongue to swell to twice its **normal** size. "You must come out!" someone finally yelled from a nearby tugboat.

Trudy raised her head and looked into the black waves. "What for?" she called back. Trudy knew this was her last, best **opportunity** to become the first woman to swim the English Channel.

When Trudy stepped into the water on August 6, 1926, few people thought the 19-year-old had a chance of swimming the Channel. The narrow sea that separates England from France is only 21 miles wide, but the tides are **treacherous**, the water is bone-chilling cold, and the weather is uncertain. The Channel was so dangerous that by 1926 only five people in history had been able to swim across it. All had been men.

The sea was a chilly 61 degrees when Trudy waded into the water off Cape Gris-Nez, France, at 7:09 A.M. She had chosen this day because the weather **forecast** was **favorable**. At 1:30 P.M., however, it started to rain. At first, the rain was gentle, but within a few hours a full-sized storm swooped across the Channel. By 5:00 P.M. the sea was rough, and the tide was running against Trudy. By 6:00 P.M. it seemed hopeless. Tom Burgess, Trudy's coach, begged her to get out of the water. But Trudy was only six miles from the English shore. "No! No! she shouted.

Trudy finally reached the beach at Kingsdown, England, at 9:40 P.M. She had been in the water for 14 hours and 31 minutes. Trudy wasn't just the first woman to swim the Channel. She had beaten the world-record time by almost two hours.

Personal Words

Choose two words from the selection that are not familiar to you or whose meanings you are not completely sure of. (Do not choose words that appear in boldfaced type.) Write the words on the lines provided. Beside each word write what you think it means, based on how it was used in the selection.

1. _____ : _____

   _____

2. _____ : _____

   _____

Using Context

A Put an **X** in the box beside the correct meaning for each boldfaced word. For clues to the meanings of the words, reread the parts of the passage in which they appear.

1. **normal**
   - ☐ a. different
   - ☐ b. unusual
   - ☐ c. usual

2. **opportunity**
   - ☐ a. good chance
   - ☐ b. reason
   - ☐ c. excuse

3. **treacherous**
   - ☐ a. dangerous
   - ☐ b. harmless
   - ☐ c. famous

4. **forecast**
   - ☐ a. review
   - ☐ b. prediction
   - ☐ c. warning

5. **favorable**
   - ☐ a. hurtful
   - ☐ b. discouraging
   - ☐ c. advantageous

B On the line beside each sentence, write the vocabulary word that has the same meaning as the underlined word or words.

| normal | opportunity | treacherous | forecast | favorable |

1. _____ Sean knew that the trail would be <u>dangerous</u> to travel at night.

2. _____ The library will be open during its <u>regular</u> hours on Saturday.

3. _____ The steady winds should provide <u>really helpful</u> conditions for the sailboat races today.

4. _____ *The Old Farmer's Almanac* is a book that provides a <u>prediction</u> of the weather for the year ahead.

5. _____ Gina was grateful for the <u>good chance</u> to coach the junior swim team.

Making Connections

A On the line next to each word or phrase, write the vocabulary word that is related to it. The related word or phrase may be a synonym, an antonym, or a definition for the vocabulary word.

normal	**opportunity**	**treacherous**	**forecast**	**favorable**

1. safe _____

2. review _____

3. good chance _____

4. unusual _____

5. harmful _____

6. dangerous _____

7. prediction _____

8. irregular _____

9. helpful _____

10. usual _____

B Complete each sentence with the correct vocabulary word.

normal	**opportunity**	**treacherous**	**forecast**	**favorable**

1. The coach said that anyone who attends every practice will have an

   _____ to make the team.

2. The early season _____ is that the Ravens will win the Super Bowl again.

3. The icy sidewalk was _____ to walk on.

4. It's not _____ for our state to have so much snow in November.

5. Luke was hoping to get a _____ report card to show his parents.

Personal Words Follow-up

Use a dictionary to help you find the definitions for the personal words you chose at the beginning of this lesson. If a word has more than one meaning, look for the meaning that defines the word as it is used in the selection. Then write the words and their dictionary definitions in the Personal Words pages at the back of the book.

22 | Word Study: Homonyms

As you read the following paragraph, pay particular attention to the boldfaced words:

> I thought you **knew** that Dad needed a **new sail** for his model sailboat. The owners of the Hobby Shop are having a **sale** today at **their** mall store. Let's go **there** and buy **two** of them. I need one for my boat **too**.

Did you notice anything unusual about the boldfaced words? Did you notice that there are four pairs of words in which the two words sound alike but have different meanings and different spellings? The pairs include (1) *knew* and *new*, (2) *sail* and *sale*, (3) *their* and *there*, and (4) *two* and *too*.

The two words in each pair are homonyms—two words that sound alike but have different meanings and, usually, different spellings. Which homonym should be used in each of the following sentences?

1. The library is having a book (**sail** or **sale**) today.
2. Chen and Bryan left (**their** or **there**) books at the library.
3. "I'm trying, but I only have (**two** or **too**) hands," said Alfrie.
4. Linda thought I (**knew** or **new**) the right answer to the question.

Did you choose these correct homonyms: *sale, their, two,* and *knew?*

Finding Meanings

Below is a list of homonyms. Choose the correct word to complete each sentence.

   brake—break   **blew—blue**   **right—write**   **cents—sense**   **ate—eight**

1. Nicole has a wonderful _____ of humor.

2. The wind _____ so strongly that it tore our kite.

3. After working for an hour, Matt took a 10-minute _____.

4. Kristen was eager to _____ to her new pen pal.

5. James still had _____ more math problems to do.

Sense and Meaning

On the lines provided, write each sentence, using the correct homonym.

1. Gwen told us a scary (**tale** or **tail**) about ghosts.

   _____

2. Many years ago most naval officers wore (**steal** or **steel**) swords.

   _____

3. Our family loves the (**peace** or **piece**) and quiet of country life.

   _____

4. The ranchers drove the (**heard** or **herd**) of cattle across the plains.

   _____

5. Vinny hasn't decided (**weather** or **whether**) he'll go with us.

   _____

6. The (**some** or **sum**) of 25 and 15 is 40.

   _____

7. The old wooden floor will (**creak** or **creek**) when you walk on it.

   _____

8. Put more (**wood** or **would**) on the fire before it goes out.

   _____

Making Connections

The boldfaced words listed below are homonyms. Match each homonym with its meaning by writing the letter of the meaning beside it.

_____ 1. **flour**　　　　a. opening in or through something

_____ 2. **flower**　　　　b. without strength

_____ 3. **weak**　　　　c. blossom part of a plant

_____ 4. **week**　　　　d. having all its parts; complete; entire

_____ 5. **hole**　　　　e. grain that is ground to a powder

_____ 6. **whole**　　　　f. period of seven days straight

23 | The Old Oaken Bucket

Visitors still stop at the old house in Scituate, Massachusetts, but the house is not what brings them there. What they want to see is the old stone well beside it—and the ironbound water bucket that is set on its edge.

Two hundred years ago, this farmhouse was the home of Samuel Woodworth. During the long summers of his childhood, young Samuel would often pause at the well. It was a welcome break, especially on a hot afternoon. On such a day he would eagerly draw a bucketful of cold water and **quench** his thirst with a refreshing drink.

When he was 14, Woodworth left Scituate. In time he traveled to New York City. There he worked at newspapers and magazines while writing novels, plays, and poetry in his spare time. Woodworth never stopped thinking of his Scituate home, however. Working in busy New York made him homesick for the peace and **solitude** of life in the country.

After work one evening in 1817, Woodworth poured himself a glass of city water. It wasn't very refreshing. **Casually** he **remarked** to his wife, Lydia, how wonderful it would be to have a long, cool drink from the oaken bucket at his father's well. Lydia had a thought. Why not put it to poetry?

It was an idea Woodworth could not **resist**. That night he wrote "The Bucket." In it he captured the world of his childhood on a hot summer day and the simple joy of stopping for a drink at his father's well. The poem was an instant success. "The Old Oaken Bucket" (as it came to be called) was translated into four languages. And the words were set to a popular tune of the time. Today it is the official song of Scituate, Massachusetts.

Personal Words

Choose two words from the selection that are not familiar to you or whose meanings you are not completely sure of. (Do not choose words that appear in boldfaced type.) Write the words on the lines provided. Beside each word write what you think it means, based on how it was used in the selection.

1. _____ : _____

   _____

2. _____ : _____

   _____

Using Context

A Put an **X** in the box beside the correct meaning for each boldfaced word. For clues to the meanings of the words, reread the parts of the passage in which they appear.

1. To **quench** one's thirst means to
   - ☐ a. make one more thirsty.
   - ☐ b. satisfy or stop one's thirst.
   - ☐ c. spray water on someone.

2. If someone **remarked** about something to you, that person would have
   - ☐ a. mentioned something to you.
   - ☐ b. shouted at you.
   - ☐ c. talked to you for a long time.

3. Someone who prefers to live in **solitude** wants to live
   - ☐ a. close to other people.
   - ☐ b. with other people.
   - ☐ c. away from other people.

4. Samuel's remark about how wonderful it would be to have a drink from the oaken bucket was made **casually**. This means that he
   - ☐ a. said it without much thinking.
   - ☐ b. carefully thought about what to say.
   - ☐ c. said it in an excited way.

5. From the sentence in which *resist* appears, you can tell that **resist** means
   - ☐ a. prefer to do.
   - ☐ b. decide what to do.
   - ☐ c. keep from doing.

B Complete each sentence with the correct vocabulary word.

quench   **remarked**   **solitude**   **casually**   **resist**

1. Stacey _____ looked through the magazine while she waited for her friend.

2. Winning the race was the only thing that would _____ Kip's desire to succeed.

3. Scott could not _____ playing a joke on Adam.

4. Rachel, who loves crowds, hated the _____ of the forest.

5. "It looks as though it's going to snow," Mr. Galvin _____ as he hurried by.

Making Connections

A The boldfaced words listed below are vocabulary words you studied in this lesson. Use one of these words to complete each of the following analogies. Remember that in an analogy, the words in the second word pair must be related to each other in the same way that the words in the first word pair are related.

| quench | remarked | solitude | casually | resist |

1. **Loud** is to **noisy** as **quiet** is to _____.

2. **Observed** is to **saw** as _____ is to **said**.

3. **Planned** is to **unintended** as **seriously** is to _____.

4. **Please** is to **delight** as **satisfy** is to _____.

5. **Allow** is to **permit** as _____ is to **fight**.

B Write each word from the list below beside its meaning. To figure out what each word means, go back to the passage and read the sentence that contains the word. If you can't discover the meaning from the way the word is used in the sentence, look for clues in the sentences that come before and after it.

| quench | remarked | solitude | casually | resist |

1. _____ said briefly

2. _____ without much thinking; offhand

3. _____ satisfy; put an end to; stop

4. _____ state of being alone; being away from others

5. _____ keep from; act or fight against

Personal Words Follow-up

Use a dictionary to help you find the definitions for the personal words you chose at the beginning of this lesson. If a word has more than one meaning, look for the meaning that defines the word as it is used in the selection. Then write the words and their dictionary definitions in the Personal Words pages at the back of the book.

The word part *tele-* means "at a distance" or "far." *Tele-* can be combined with other words or word parts to form new words such as *telescope* and *television*. Knowing the meaning of *tele-* will help you figure out the meanings of many other words. For example, *phone* means "sound," so a telephone is an instrument that reproduces sounds at a distance. Study the table below to see how some word parts are combined to form new words.

Word Part	Word or Word Part	Word
tele- (far, at a distance)	+ scope (instrument for viewing)	= telescope
tele- (far, at a distance)	+ vision (seeing)	= television
micro- (very small)	+ scope (instrument for viewing)	= microscope
peri- (around)	+ scope (instrument for viewing)	= periscope
trans- (across)	+ port (carry)	= transport
trans- (across)	+ -mit (send)	= transmit

Notice that the word *microscope* was formed by combining *micro-* with *scope*. The meaning of *micro-* combines with the meaning of *scope* to give the meaning of the word *microscope*—"an instrument for seeing very small things." A telescope is an instrument for seeing distant, or faraway, objects. What is a periscope in a submarine used for? Yes, to see around the surface of the sea. Can you figure out the meanings of the words *transport, television,* and *transmit*?

Finding Meanings

Write each boldfaced word or word part beside its meaning.

port   **tele-**   **micro-**   **-mit**   **vision**

1. send _____

2. very small _____

3. far; at a distance _____

4. seeing _____

5. carry _____

Sense and Meaning

Complete each sentence by using a word from the Word
column in the table on page 86. Be sure that the word makes
sense in the sentence.

1. Jay could see the North Star clearly by looking through his _____.

2. A bus will _____ the band to the football game.

3. The game is too far away to attend, but we'll see it on _____.

4. The ship's captain tried to _____ a warning message to the small
   boat.

5. The scientist used a _____ to study the tiny germs.

Making Connections

Each of the boldfaced words contains a word or word part you
have studied in this lesson. Beside each word write the word or
word part and its meaning.

	Word or Word Part	**Meaning**
1. **portable**	_____	_____
2. **telephone**	_____	_____
3. **remit**	_____	_____
4. **import**	_____	_____
5. **revision**	_____	_____
6. **telegraph**	_____	_____
7. **visionary**	_____	_____
8. **horoscope**	_____	_____
9. **microfilm**	_____	_____
10. **admit**	_____	_____

21-24 | Review and Extension

Finding Meanings

A The boldfaced words listed below are vocabulary words you studied in lessons 21 and 23. Use each word correctly in a sentence to show that you know the meaning of the word.

1. **solitude** _____

_____

2. **forecast** _____

_____

3. **casually** _____

_____

4. **opportunity** _____

_____

5. **resist** _____

_____

6. **treacherous** _____

_____

B The boldfaced words listed below are homonyms you studied in Lesson 22. Complete each sentence with the correct homonym. Use what you learned about homonyms in that lesson to help you.

knew—new   sail—sale   there—their   too—two   brake—break

1. It took great courage for the Pilgrims to _____ to America.

2. Lewis had to use his _____ quickly to stop his bike in time.

3. Corinne hung your jacket on the chair over _____.

4. It was raining _____ hard for the outdoor concert to continue.

5. They are building a _____ middle school in our neighborhood.

88

Sense and Meaning

The words and word parts you worked with in lesson 24 are
listed below. Beside each word that follows, write the words and
word parts that make up the word. Then write the word in a
sentence on the line provided. Be sure that the word makes
sense in the sentence.

peri-	trans-	micro-	-mit
port	scope	tele-	vision

1. **transport** _____ _____

_____

2. **microscope** _____ _____

_____

3. **television** _____ _____

_____

4. **periscope** _____ _____

_____

5. **transmit** _____ _____

_____

6. **telescope** _____ _____

_____

Synonym Study

Following are synonym studies for two vocabulary words you
studied in lessons 21 and 23. Use either the vocabulary words
or their synonyms to complete the sentences in this exercise.
Check with the synonym studies as you decide which choice
best fits the context of each sentence.

forecast   predict

The words *forecast*, as a verb, and *predict* both mean "tell ahead of time what will happen
in the future." The word *forecast* is generally used when one first makes a careful study
of known facts before stating what will happen in the future. *The Weather Service forecast
heavy rain for tomorrow.* The word *predict* suggests that someone's personal knowledge
and experience as well as some kind of scientific study are involved in arriving at a
conclusion about future events. *Scientists can now predict when some volcanoes will erupt, or
burst. Predict* is often used in a much more general sense. *Nat said, "I predict that my dad
will not let me camp out alone in the woods tonight."* In this example, Nat uses only his
knowledge of his dad and his experience with him to help him predict whether his dad
will permit him to camp out.

1. Knowing her as I do, I _____ that Ann won't run for class
   president.

2. The experts _____ a large increase in jobs in our country next year.

solitude   seclusion

The words *solitude* and *seclusion* both mean "the state of being alone." *Solitude* expresses
the idea of the quiet and peace of being alone. *Jenna enjoyed the solitude of the mountain
for a few days, but then she began to miss her family.* The word *seclusion* suggests the idea of
shutting oneself away from other people on purpose. *Joel lives in seclusion now, and does
not see any of his old friends.*

3. The former governor went into _____ after he was accused of
   receiving bribes.

4. Mike loved the _____ of the small, uncrowded lake.

Word Forms

The boldfaced words listed below are other forms of the vocabulary words you studied in lessons 21, 23, and 24. Fill in the blank in each sentence with the proper word. If you are unsure of the meaning of a word, look it up in the glossary.

favorably   **quenching**   **televise**   **resistance**   **transmitting**

remarkable   **forecaster**   **casual**   **normally**   **opportunities**

1. Mr. Lopez works as a _____ for the Weather Service.

2. Channel 5 is going to _____ the Thanksgiving Day Parade.

3. Our school is _____ closed the day after Thanksgiving.

4. My mother had a _____ meeting with my teacher at the supermarket today.

5. The astronauts continued _____ information to the scientists on Earth.

6. Missy's singing performance was so _____, that people are still talking about it.

7. Our science teacher said that we would all be given many _____ to earn extra credit.

8. The firefighters were successful in _____ the fire in the building.

9. The town council voted _____ on the request to build a new playground.

10. There was no _____ to the council's decision to build a new playground.

92

Using Your Vocabulary

Use vocabulary words introduced in lessons 21–24 to complete this word puzzle. For each definition or synonym in column A, think of a vocabulary word that has the same meaning. Then in column B, spell out the vocabulary word in the spaces beside its meaning. One or two letters are provided for each word.

Column A

Column B

1. satisfy; stop ___ u ___ n ___ ___

2. keep from doing ___ ___ s ___ ___ ___

3. state of being alone s ___ ___ ___ ___ ___ ___ e

4. carry across ___ ___ a ___ ___ p ___ ___ ___

5. statement telling what will happen ___ o ___ ___ ___ ___ ___ t

6. instrument for seeing distant objects t ___ ___ ___ ___ ___ ___ p ___

7. without serious thought ___ ___ s ___ ___ l ___ ___

8. said in a few words; commented ___ ___ ___ a r ___ ___ ___ ___

9. usual; regular ___ ___ ___ ___ ___ l

10. instrument used to see very small things ___ ___ c ___ ___ s ___ ___ ___ ___

11. good chance ___ ___ ___ o ___ t ___ ___ ___ ___ ___

12. send across ___ ___ ___ ___ s ___ ___ t

13. helpful ___ ___ ___ o ___ ___ ___ ___ e

14. dangerous ___ r ___ ___ ___ ___ ___ r ___ ___ ___

15. instrument used to see images sent from far away ___ e ___ ___ ___ ___ ___ i ___ ___

25 | The Wandering Albatross

The wandering albatross is a famous and mysterious bird that few of us ever see. Its fame began with sea stories in the days of sailing ships. Those few sailors who **ventured** into the stormy waters of the southern oceans had a story to tell. Their ships might be followed for days, even for weeks, by an albatross gliding close behind.

Here are a few facts about this **unique** bird. The wandering albatross is the largest in the family of seabirds. It weighs about 20 pounds, and it has a wingspan of 10 feet or more. Its long, narrow wings are better for gliding than for flapping.

The wandering albatross has no known enemies. It has no fear of people, so it has been easy to study on land. But how do you study the birds while they are wandering over the oceans?

Two French scientists figured out how to track the wandering albatross on its long flights. They put little radio transmitters on several birds. Radio receivers on two satellites helped the scientists to locate where the birds were. **Observations** from the satellites were sent to computers in France. The scientists used the information to draw a map of each bird's flight path.

By day the wandering albatross travels distances of up to 600 miles. At night flights are much shorter. The birds often stop to rest on the water, but they never stop for longer than a few hours at a time. The wandering albatross certainly lives up to its **reputation** as a wanderer. Scientists still do not know how the birds **navigate** without any signs or landmarks to guide their way.

Personal Words

Choose two words from the selection that are not familiar to you or whose meanings you are not completely sure of. (Do not choose words that appear in boldfaced type.) Write the words on the lines provided. Beside each word write what you think it means, based on how it was used in the selection.

1. _____ : _____

_____

2. _____ : _____

_____

94

Using Context

A Put an **X** in the box beside the correct meaning for each boldfaced word. For clues to the meanings of the words, reread the parts of the passage in which they appear.

1. Long ago, sailors who **ventured** into the southern oceans returned with stories of a mysterious bird.
   - ☐ a. dared to go
   - ☐ b. refused to go
   - ☐ c. asked to go

2. Scientific studies have shown that this is an interesting bird with a **unique** way of life.
   - ☐ a. very familiar
   - ☐ b. highly common
   - ☐ c. most unusual

3. **Observations** from the satellites were sent to computers in France.
   - ☐ a. space rockets
   - ☐ b. information obtained by seeing or noticing
   - ☐ c. objects put into space to gather information

4. The wandering albatross certainly lives up to its **reputation** as a wanderer.
   - ☐ a. an ability to fly
   - ☐ b. general knowledge or feeling about someone or something
   - ☐ c. an amazing memory

5. The scientists still do not know how the birds **navigate** without any signs or landmarks to guide their way.
   - ☐ a. follow a course
   - ☐ b. rest on the water
   - ☐ c. fly so high

B Write each word from the list below beside its meaning. To figure out what each word means, go back to the passage and read the sentence that contains the word. If you can't discover the meaning from the way the word is used in the sentence, look for clues in the sentences that come before and after it.

ventured	unique	observations	reputation	navigate

1. _____ highly uncommon; rare; one of a kind

2. _____ general knowledge or feeling about someone or something

3. _____ did something involving risk

4. _____ to direct or follow a course through, on, or over

5. _____ acts of examining and noting facts

Making Connections

A On the line beside each sentence, write the vocabulary word that has the same meaning as the underlined word or words.

> **ventured**   **unique**   **observations**   **reputation**   **navigate**

1. _____ The captain was able to <u>direct the course of</u> his ship through the narrow canal.

2. _____ The largest living bird is the ostrich, a <u>rare, one-of-a-kind</u> bird that can run but cannot fly.

3. _____ The trainer <u>attempted the dangerous job of going</u> into the lion's cage alone.

4. _____ Scientists have shared their <u>acts of examining and noting facts</u> about the habits of whales.

5. _____ The <u>general feeling or opinion</u> of their grocery store is very important to the Wongs.

B Complete each sentence with the correct vocabulary word.

> **ventured**   **unique**   **observations**   **reputation**   **navigate**

1. After the careful _____ of several doctors, Carrie learned that she had a heart problem.

2. Each of the judges has a _____ for being fair and honest.

3. A few brave people have _____ across the Atlantic Ocean in an open hot-air balloon.

4. A ride in a hot-air balloon would be a _____ experience for most people.

5. Bus drivers _____ their vehicles on busy city streets.

Personal Words Follow-up

Use a dictionary to help you find the definitions for the personal words you chose at the beginning of this lesson. If a word has more than one meaning, look for the meaning that defines the word as it is used in the selection. Then write the words and their dictionary definitions in the Personal Words pages at the back of the book.

26 Word Study: Context Clues

In lesson 22 you learned that homonyms are words that sound alike but have different meanings and usually different spellings. Examples are: *sail* and *sale* and *knew* and *new*. In this lesson, you will learn about another interesting type of word. Read the following sentence and pay particular attention to the boldfaced words:

I saw the **dove** just before it **dove** to the ground.

Did you notice that the two words are spelled exactly alike? Do they both have the same meaning? No, the first *dove* is a noun, meaning "a bird of the pigeon family." The second *dove* is a verb, meaning "went down suddenly." Did you notice that the two words do not sound alike? The correct pronunciation of each word is given below with a special spelling right after the word, such as you'll find in the glossary at the back of your book.

a. **dove (duv)**, a bird
b. **dov (dōv)**, went down suddenly

Words such as *dove* (duv) and *dove* (dōv) are spelled the same way but have different meanings and different pronunciations. The context in which the word appears will help you decide its meaning. The correct meaning of the word will also tell you which pronunciation to use. A dictionary can help you with both the meaning and the pronunciations of words.

Finding Meanings

Write the letter of the correct pronunciation and meaning of each boldfaced word on the line beside the sentence.

_____ 1. Marty caught a six-pound **bass** at the lake today.

        a. (bās), a low male voice   b. (bas), a kind of fish

_____ 2. The **wind** was much too strong for flying our kites today.

        a. (wind), air in motion   b. (wīnd), to turn

_____ 3. The ranger warned us to not stand too **close** to the animal cages.

        a. (klōz), to shut   b. (klōs), near

_____ 4. The gym teacher asked us to stand in a straight **row**.

        a. (rō), line of people   b. (rou), a noisy quarrel or fight

Sense and Meaning

Put an **X** in the box beside the correct pronunciation and meaning of the boldfaced word in each sentence.

1. The **bow** was damaged when it hit the dock.
   - ☐ a. (bō), a weapon for shooting arrows
   - ☐ b. (bou), the forward part of a ship or boat

2. After the engine quit, Jerry had to **row** back to shore.
   - ☐ a. (rō), to use oars to move a boat
   - ☐ b. (rou), a noisy quarrel or fight

3. Lisa couldn't wait to **tear** open the package she got for her birthday.
   - ☐ a. (tār), to pull apart
   - ☐ b. (tēr), a liquid from the eye

4. The little boy dreamed of one day owning a real **live** pony.
   - ☐ a. (liv), to be alive; to exist
   - ☐ b. (līv), having life; living

5. We quietly watched as two **does** drank water from the forest brook.
   - ☐ a. (dōz), more than one adult female deer
   - ☐ b. (duz), present tense of the verb *to do*

Making Connections

Match each boldfaced word below with its meaning by writing the letter of the meaning beside the word. The pronunciation of each word will help you determine its meaning. If you need more help, use the glossary at the back of the book.

_____ 1. **dove (dōv)**	a.	to shut
_____ 2. **close (klōs)**	b.	to bend in greeting or respect
_____ 3. **bow (bō)**	c.	went down suddenly
_____ 4. **close (klōz)**	d.	a bird
_____ 5. **dove (duv)**	e.	a weapon for shooting arrows with
_____ 6. **bow (bou)**	f.	near

27 | Albert Comes Home!

Ever lose something and then later find it in the most unexpected way? Well that's happened quite a few times to astronomers. Except, the things they've lost haven't been their car keys. They've been asteroids, **minor** planets **orbiting** the sun.

Now, just how can you lose a big hunk of rock spinning through space? Easy. Space is very big, and compared to space, the "rocks" are very small. If you don't get a good fix on their position as they move . . . well, asteroids can disappear.

And that's what happened in 1911 when Austrian astronomer Johann Palisa discovered asteroid 719, which he named Albert. The asteroid was followed for a month as it drifted through space. The astronomers thought they had figured out a fairly good orbit for it. That's important, because as asteroids round the sun, their brightness becomes stronger and then weaker.

When the asteroid is far from Earth, we can't see and follow it. That's where **precise** observations come in handy. If the asteroid's orbit is known precisely, astronomers can **calculate** where and when it will return to sight.

Alas, poor Albert rounded the sun in 1911, faded from sight, and never returned. Other asteroids have been lost this way too. But as of 1911, all of them had been **recovered**. Albert was the last "missing" asteroid. Then, in May 2000, the Spacewatch telescope in Arizona spotted and tracked a faint asteroid. Soon after, Gareth Williams of the Minor Planet Center at the Harvard-Smithsonian Center for Astrophysics in Cambridge, Massachusetts, was able to prove that it was the missing Albert. "It's been a long time," Williams said, "but I'm very glad I got it."

Now that we've got the fix on Albert, you can be sure we won't lose it again.

Personal Words

Choose two words from the selection that are not familiar to you or whose meanings you are not completely sure of. (Do not choose words that appear in boldfaced type.) Write the words on the lines provided. Beside each word write what you think it means, based on how it was used in the selection.

1. _____ : _____

_____

2. _____ : _____

_____

Using Context

A Put an **X** in the box beside the correct meaning for each boldfaced word. For clues to the meanings of the words, reread the parts of the passage in which they appear.

1. After reading the article "Albert Comes Home!" you can tell from the context that **minor** means
   - ☐ a. very important.
   - ☐ b. not very important.
   - ☐ c. big and thick

2. Minor planets that are **orbiting** the sun are traveling
   - ☐ a. directly toward the sun.
   - ☐ b. around the sun.
   - ☐ c. directly away from the sun.

3. When astronomers make **precise** observations, they make observations that are
   - ☐ a. exact.
   - ☐ b. useful.
   - ☐ c. interesting.

4. The sentence in which **calculate** appears helps you to understand that in this context *calculate* means to
   - ☐ a. see something through a telescope.
   - ☐ b. take photographs.
   - ☐ c. figure out something by using mathematics.

5. From the sentence in which **recovered** appears, you can tell that *recovered* means
   - ☐ a. got well.
   - ☐ b. got damaged.
   - ☐ c. got back something lost.

B Complete each sentence with the correct vocabulary word.

minor	orbiting	precise	calculate	recovered

1. My dad has to _____ the cost of building a porch for our house.

2. To set her new clock correctly, Eve needed to know the _____ time.

3. Jody will play on a _____ league team until he's old enough to play on a regular Little League team.

4. The space station has been _____ Earth for almost two years.

5. Jake _____ his baseball glove that he thought had been lost.

Making Connections

A The boldfaced words listed below are vocabulary words you studied in this lesson. Use one of these words to complete each of the following analogies. Remember that in an analogy, the words in the second word pair must be related to each other in the same way that the words in the first word pair are related.

minor   orbiting   precise   calculate   recovered

1. **Right** is to **correct** as **exact** is to _____.

2. **Captured** is to **released** as **lost** is to _____.

3. **Greater** is to **major** as **lesser** is to _____.

4. **Down** is to **diving** as **around** is to _____.

5. **Realize** is to **understand** as **figure** is to _____.

B Write each word from the list below beside its meaning. To figure out what each word means, go back to the passage and read the sentence that contains the word. If you can't discover the meaning from the way the word is used in the sentence, look for clues in the sentences that come before and after it.

minor   orbiting   precise   calculate   recovered

1. _____ got back something lost or stolen

2. _____ traveling around another body in space

3. _____ determine through the use of mathematics

4. _____ not very important

5. _____ accurate; exact

Personal Words Follow-up

Use a dictionary to help you find the definitions for the personal words you chose at the beginning of this lesson. If a word has more than one meaning, look for the meaning that defines the word as it is used in the selection. Then write the words and their dictionary definitions in the Personal Words pages at the back of the book.

28 | Word Study: Figures of Speech

Writers often make their work interesting by using special comparisons. These special ways of comparing unlike people or things are called figures of speech. Most figures of speech compare a person or a thing to something else in one particular way. One kind of figure of speech uses the words *like* or *as* to show that two different things are alike in some way. Read the following sentences.

Karen swims <u>like a fish</u>.
Mike is <u>as quiet as a mouse</u> at school.

These comparisons give you a good idea of how well Karen swims and how quiet Mike is. In another kind of figure of speech, a person or a thing is said to *be* something else.

"He may be fast on a basketball court," said his mother, "but <u>Jim is a turtle</u> when it comes to doing his chores."

Do you think his mother meant that Jim is really a turtle? Of course she didn't. That wouldn't make any sense. She meant that Jim is as slow as a turtle when it comes to doing his chores.

If you think a writer is using a figure of speech, first decide what two things the writer is comparing. Then use the context to help you decide in what way the writer means that the two things are alike.

Finding Meanings

Two possible meanings are given for the underlined figure of speech in each sentence. On the line next to the sentence, write the letter of the correct meaning. Use the context to help you.

_____ 1. During the summer, the attic room was <u>a furnace</u>.

   a. the room was very hot   b. the room was on fire

_____ 2. The icy rain was <u>like needles</u> striking Mira's face.

   a. the rain stuck into Mira's face   b. the rain stung Mira's face

_____ 3. Luis is <u>like a cat</u> when he plays shortstop on our baseball team.

   a. Luis's hands are like paws   b. Luis is quick on his feet

_____ 4. When she saw her birthday cake, Liz's eyes were <u>as big as saucers</u>.

   a. Liz's eyes were open wide   b. Liz's eyes were flat

Sense and Meaning

A figure of speech is used in each sentence below. On the lines
provided, write the names of the two things being compared.
Then explain how the two things are thought to be alike.

1. On a clear night, the stars are like diamonds in the sky.

   _____ / _____

   _____

2. After two days of heavy rain, our backyard was a lake.

   _____ / _____

   _____

3. Becky cooked the fudge too long, and now it is as hard as a rock.

   _____ / _____

   _____

4. The teacher told Sue Ann to stop being a grasshopper and to sit down.

   _____ / _____

   _____

Making Connections

Each sentence below contains a figure of speech. Decide how
the two things being compared are thought to be alike. Write
the letter of the meaning beside each sentence.

_____ 1. Brenda kept brushing until her hair was like silk.

_____ 2. During Miss Lopez's art lesson, our classroom is a beehive.

_____ 3. The clouds were giant cotton balls drifting by.

_____ 4. In the dark, the car's headlights were like cat's eyes.

a. Both are round.

b. Both are full of activity.

c. Both are fluffy and white.

d. Both are used to make cloth.

e. Both are full of bees.

f. Both glow brightly.

g. Both are shiny and smooth.

h. Both come in pairs.

25-28 | Review and Extension

Finding Meanings

A The boldfaced words listed below are vocabulary words you studied in lessons 25 and 27. Match each word with its meaning by writing the letter of its meaning beside each word.

_____	1. **navigate**	a.	did something involving risk
_____	2. **minor**	b.	traveling around another body in space
_____	3. **observations**	c.	follow a course through, on, or over
_____	4. **precise**	d.	unusual; highly uncommon; rare
_____	5. **ventured**	e.	determine through the use of mathematics
_____	6. **recovered**	f.	not very important
_____	7. **orbiting**	g.	acts of noting and recording facts
_____	8. **reputation**	h.	got back something lost or stolen
_____	9. **unique**	i.	accurate; exact
_____	10. **calculate**	j.	what people think of someone or something

B Two pronunciations are given for each boldfaced word below. Write the letter of the correct pronunciation on the line beside each sentence.

_____ 1. "Be sure to **close** the door on your way out," Mother warned.

  a. (klōz)   b. (klōs)

_____ 2. The hawk circled once and then **dove** back to its perch in the tree.

  a. (duv)   b. (dōv)

_____ 3. Mrs. Young asked Manuel if he would sing **bass** in the school choir.

  a. (bas)   b. (bās)

_____ 4. The Swiss hero William Tell was an expert with a **bow** and arrow.

a. (bō) b. (bou)

_____ 5. The movie was so sad that Ann had to wipe a **tear** from her eye.

a. (tār) b. (tēr)

Sense and Meaning

A figure of speech is underlined in each of the following sentences. State in your own words what the figure of speech means by rewriting each sentence on the lines provided. Remember, first decide what two things are being compared. Then explain how the two things are thought to be alike.

1. The rabbit stood <u>like a statue</u>, hoping the dog wouldn't see it.

_____

_____

2. Pamela didn't sleep well at summer camp because her bed was <u>as hard as a wooden board</u>.

_____

_____

3. After weeks without any rain, our vegetable garden is <u>a desert</u>.

_____

_____

4. Our cat is lazy, but she moves <u>like lightning</u> when I put her food dish down.

_____

_____

5. When Dad asked Mikey how the bowl got broken, Mikey just stood there <u>like a stone</u>.

_____

_____

6. The lights from the city are <u>a rainbow</u> in the nighttime sky.

_____

_____

Synonym Study

Following are synonym studies for two vocabulary words you studied in lessons 25 and 27. Use either the vocabulary words or their synonyms to complete the sentences in this exercise. Refer to the synonym studies as you decide which choice best fits the context of each sentence.

venture   **dare**

Both *venture* and *dare* mean "to have the necessary bravery or courage to do something." The word *venture* expresses the idea of willingly taking a chance to do something that involves risk or danger, especially something that is important. *Astronauts continue to venture out into deep space.* The word *dare* suggests being bold enough to do something dangerous or risky. *I wouldn't dare try to climb Mt. Everest.*

1. The early pioneers had to _____ across wild and unknown lands to start a new life in the West.

2. I asked Tom if he would _____ to go into the old haunted house on Halloween night.

precise   **correct**

The words *precise* and *correct* both mean "to be free from mistake or error." *Correct* is the word generally used to mean "mistake or error-free." *Millie had the correct answer for every question on the test.* The word *precise* stresses the idea of being not only correct and accurate in every detail but also clearly and definitely stated. *Because Mr. Silver's directions were so precise, we had no trouble finding his farm.*

3. "Do you have Sandy's _____ telephone number?" asked Carol.

4. Only mother knows the _____ amount of sugar to use in that recipe.

Word Forms

The boldfaced words listed below are other forms of the
vocabulary words you studied in lessons 25 and 27. Complete
each sentence with the correct word. If you are unsure of the
meaning of a word, look it up in the glossary.

recovery	**precision**	**navigation**	**venturesome**	**minority**
uniquely	**navigator**	**observatory**	**calculator**	**orbit**

1. Before he could sail his boat across the ocean, Mr. Maheen had to pass a course in

   _____.

2. All the planets in the solar system _____ the sun.

3. An astronaut is _____ prepared to teach a course in space travel.

4. An _____ is a place where scientists use telescopes to study the planets and stars.

5. Scientists measure the distance between Earth and other planets with great

   _____.

6. Only people who are _____ would skydive.

7. The Coast Guard hoped to make a full _____ of the boat that was lost in the storm.

8. Harold used his _____ to make sure that he had added the numbers correctly.

9. Only a _____ of parents did not attend the school play.

10. A _____ was brought on board to steer the ship into the harbor.

Using Your Vocabulary

Listed below under ACROSS and DOWN are numbered
definitions of 10 vocabulary words from lessons 25 and 27.
Fill in the squares in the crossword puzzle by spelling out the
vocabulary words that fit the definitions.

ACROSS
2. move through, on, or over
4. not very important
6. determine through the use of arithmetic
9. got back something lost or stolen
10. traveling around another body in space

DOWN
1. did something involving risk
3. accurate; exact
5. acts of noting and recording facts
7. unusual; highly uncommon
8. what people think about a person or thing

Personal Words

Word	Definition

Word

Definition

Word	Definition

Word

Definition

Word   **Definition**

Glossary

Pronunciation Key

Symbol	Example	Symbol	Example
a	pan	o͞o	mood
ā	make	o͝o	took
âr	dare	u	cut
ä	father	ûr	purple
e	get	yo͞o	mute
ē	seem	th	then
i	pit	th	thin
ī	ice	hw	what
îr	pier	zh	usual
o	cot	ə	about
ō	go		listen
ô	awful		pencil
oi	soil		common
ou	mouth		campus

Stress marks: ′(primary); ′(secondary) as in (vō·kab′ yə·ler′ ē)

A

accomplish (ə·kom′ plish) *v.* To succeed in completing or carrying out.

accomplishment (ə·kom′ plish·mənt) *n.* (1) An act of accomplishing. (2) Something done successfully.

accumulate (ə·kyo͞om′ yə·lāt′) *v.* To collect or pile up; to increase in amount. **accumulated**

accumulation (ə·kyo͞om′ yə·lā′ shən) *n.* That which has accumulated; a collection.

accurate (ak′ yər·it) *adj.* Exactly right; correct. *adv.* **accurately**

achieve (ə·chēv′) *v.* To succeed in gaining.

admit (ad·mit′) *v.* (1) To allow in; to permit entrance. (2) To allow the possibility of.

agreement (ə·grē′ mənt) *n.* An understanding reached by two or more parties.

allege (ə·lej′) *v.* To state or declare without proof.

alleged (ə·lejd′) *adj.* Not proved; supposed.

amass (ə·mas′) *v.* To collect a great quantity.

amazement (ə·māz′ mənt) *n.* The state or condition of being confused and surprised.

analogy (ə·nal′ ə·jē) *n.* A likeness between things that are otherwise not alike.

appoint (ə·point′) *v.* To name or select for an office or position. **appointed**

appointment (ə·point′ mənt) *n.* Selection.

assistance (ə·sis′ təns) *n.* Help; aid.

assistant (ə·sis′ tənt) *n.* A helper.

assured (ə·shŏŏrd′) *adj.* Made certain; undoubted; guaranteed. **assuring**

ate (āt) *v.* Past tense of *to eat.*

authorities (ə·thôr′ i·tēs) *n.* Experts on some subject.

authorize (ô′ thə·rīz′) *v.* To give official approval.

B

balance (bal′ əns) *n.* (1) An instrument for weighing. (2) The part of a sum of money that is left over. (3) A steady position.

bank (bangk) *n.* (1) The ground bordering a river or lake. (2) A place where money is kept. (3) A long pile or heap.

bass (bas) *n.* A kind of freshwater or saltwater fish.

bass (bās) *n.* The lowest male singing voice.

bay (bā) *n.* (1) A part of a sea partially enclosed by land. (2) A reddish-brown horse. (3) A long, deep barking sound.

believable (bi·lēv′ ə·bəl) *adj.* Worthy of being accepted as true.

blaze (blāz) *n.* (1) A bright fire. (2) A mark made on a tree. (3) A bright display.

blew (blōō) *v.* Past tense of *to blow.*

blue (blōō) *n.* The primary color between green and violet in the color spectrum.

bow (bō) *n.* A weapon for shooting arrows with.

bow (bou) *n.* The forward part of a ship or boat.

brake (brāk) *n.* A device for slowing or stopping the motion of a wheel or vehicle.

break (brāk) *n.* A brief rest period; a pause.

break (brāk) *v.* (1) To come apart. (2) To fail to keep. (3) To train to obey.

brighten (brīt′ n) *v.* To make or cause to be bright or brighter.

C

calculate (kal′ kyə·lāt′) *v.* To figure out something by using mathematics.

calculator (kal′ kyə·lā′ tər) *n.* A machine for performing mathematical operations.

casual (kazh′ ōō ·əl) *adj.* Without much thinking; offhand. *adv.* **casually**

catch (katch) *n.* A ball game. *v.* (1) To take hold of. (2) To surprise; to discover suddenly or unexpectantly.

caution (kô′ shən) *v.* To warn. *n.* Care with regard to danger or risk.

cautious (kô′ shəs) *adj.* Careful.

cents (sents) *n.* More than one cent, a coin worth one-hundredth of a dollar.

checkbook (chek′ bŏŏk′) *n.* A book containing blank checks.

childish (chīl′ dish) *adj.* Like a child.

close (klos) *adj.* Near.

close (klōz) *v.* To shut.

cloudless (kloud′ lis) *adj.* Without clouds.

compact (kəm·pakt′) *v.* To press together closely and firmly; to pack. **compacted**

compose (kəm·pōz′) *v.* To make up or form from other parts; to create a written work. **composed**

composition (kom′ pə·zish′ ən) *n.* (1) An essay or report, especially for school. (2) The manner in which something is put together; makeup; ingredients.

conceal (kən·sēl′) *v.* To hide; to keep out of sight. **concealing, concealed**

conclude (kən klōōd′) *v.* To reach a decision or opinion after careful study. **concluded**

conclusion (kən·klōō′ zhən) *n.* Final decision.

confidence (kon′ fi·dəns) *n.* Firm trust; feeling of certainty.

confident (kon′ fi·dənt) *adj.* Certain; sure.

construct (kən·strukt′) *v.* To put together; to build. **constructed**

construction (kən·struk′ shən) *n.* The action or process of building or putting together.

consult (kən·sult′) *v.* To ask for help or advice. **consulted**

convince (kən·vins′) *v.* To show the truth of something; to cause someone to believe.

correct (kə·rekt′) *adj.* Free from mistakes or errors.

crash (krash) *n.* Sudden loud noise. *v.* (1) To fall or break with force. (2) To fail to work.

creak (krēk) *v.* To make a sharp, grating, or squeaking sound.

creek (krēk) *n.* A small stream.

curable (kyoor′ ə·bəl) *adj.* Able to be cured.

D

dangerous (dān′ jər·əs) *adj.* Full of danger; risky.

dare (dār) *v.* To have boldness or courage to do or try something.

daybreak (dā′ brāk′) *n.* The time of morning when daylight first appears.

decide (di·sīd′) *v.* To make a judgment after thinking about something for some time.

definitely (def′ ə·nit·lē) *adv.* Certainly; surely.

destruction (di·struk′ shən) *n.* Great damage; condition of being destroyed.

determine (di·tûr′ min) *v.* To make a firm judgment about.

detest (di·test′) *v.* To greatly dislike; to hate.

detestable (di·tes′ tə·bəl) *adj.* Deserving to be greatly disliked.

differ (dif′ ər) *v.* To be unlike; to vary.

difference (dif′ ər·əns) *n.* The quality of being unlike or different.

differently (dif′ ər·ənt·ly) *adv.* Not in the same way.

disaster (di·zas′ tər) *n.* Any event causing great distress, suffering, or loss.

disastrous (di·zas′ trəs) *adj.* Causing or accompanied by disaster.

disconnect (dis′ kə·nekt′) *v.* To break the connection of.

dishonest (dis·on′ ist) *adj.* Not fair or truthful.

dishwasher (dish′ wosh′ ər) *n.* A machine used for washing dishes.

dislike (dis·līk′) *v.* To have a feeling of not liking.

disprove (dis·proov′) *v.* To prove to be false or incorrect.

does (dōs) *n.* More than one adult female deer.

does (duz) *v.* Present tense of the verb *to do*.

domestic (də·mes′ tik) *adj.* Tame.

dove (dōv) *v.* Went down suddenly; past tense of *to dive*.

dove (duv) *n.* Bird of the pigeon family.

driftwood (drift′ wood′) *n.* Wood floating or washed ashore.

duck (duk) *n.* A large wild bird. *v.* To lower the head or body suddenly.

dwell (dwel) *v.* To live in.

dwelling (dwel′ ing) *n.* A place to live in; home.

E

eight (āt) *n.* The cardinal number that is one more than seven.

endure (en·door′) *v.* (1) To suffer or hold out against. (2) To continue to be; to last.

enduring (en·door′ ing) *adj.* Lasting; continuing.

enough (i·nuf′) *adj.* As much or as many as needed or desired.

eventual (i·ven′ choo·əl) *adj.* Resulting from events that came before.

eventually (i·ven′ choo ·ə lē) *adv.* In the end, finally.

evidence (ev′ i·dəns) *n*. A sign or a clue; facts that indicate that something is true or false.

evident (ev′ i·dənt) *adj*. Easily seen or understood.

excitement (ik·sīt′ mənt) *n*. The state or condition of being excited.

exist (ig·zist′) *v*. To have reality; to be real.

existence (ig·zis′ təns) *n*. Being real; state of being.

extinct (ik·stingkt′) *adj*. No longer in existence.

extinction (ik·stingk′ shən) *n*. The state or condition of being or becoming extinct.

extract (ik·strakt′) *v*. To pull out. **extracted**

eyesight (ī′ sīt) *n*. Ability to see.

F

famous (fā′ məs) *adj*. Having fame; well-known.

fauna (fô′ nə) *n*. Animals.

favorable (fā′ vər·ə·bəl) *adj*. In one's favor; helpful. *adv*. **favorably**

fearful (fîr′ fəl) *adj*. Full of fear; afraid.

fixable (fiks′ ə·bəl) *adj*. Able to be fixed.

flour (flour) *n*. Grain that is ground to a powder.

flower (flour) *n*. The blossom part of a plant.

foolish (foo′ lish) *adj*. Like a fool; silly.

footprints (foot′ prints′) *n*. Marks made by feet.

forecast (for′ kast′) *n*. A statement telling what will happen; a prediction. *v*. To predict on the basis of careful study. *n*. **forecaster**

foreleg (fôr′ leg′) *n*. One of the front legs of a four-legged animal.

foresee (fôr·sē′) *v*. To know before; to know about the future.

foretell (fôr·tel′) *v*. To tell before in time; to tell about the future.

frail (frāl) *adj*. Weak.

G

grade (grād) *n*. (1) A mark received for schoolwork. (2) A class in school. (3) Slope. *v*. (1) To give a rating mark for a student's work. (2) To make smooth or level.

grapevine (grāp′ vīn′) *n*. A vine on which grapes grow.

H

handmade (hand′ mād′) *adj*. Made by hand rather than by machine.

harbor (här′ bər) *v*. (1) To give shelter. (2) To keep in the mind. *n*. A shelter for ships.

heard (hûrd) *v*. Past tense of *to hear*.

herd (hûrd) *n*. A group of animals of a single kind kept together.

hinder (hin′ dər) *v*. To delay; to stop.

hole (hōl) *n*. A hollow place in a solid surface.

homesick (hōm′ sik) *adj*. Unhappy about being away from one's home or family.

homeward (hōm′ wərd) *adv*. In the direction of or toward home.

homonym (hom′ ə·nim) *n*. Words that sound alike but have different meanings and usually different spellings.

hopeless (hōp′ lis) *adj*. Without hope.

horoscope (hôr′ ə·skōp) *n*. Prediction about one's future according to birthdate, often with advice.

humorous (hyoo′ mər·əs) *adj*. Full of humor; funny; comical.

I

idiom (id′ ē·əm) *n.* Words or phrases that have meanings quite different from the literal or usual meanings of the words.

illegal (i·lē′ gəl) *adj.* Not legal; unlawful.

impolite (im′ pə·līt′) *adj.* Not having good manners; rude.

import (im·pōrt′) *v.* To bring in from an outside source.

impossible (im·pos′ ə·bəl) *adj.* Not capable of happening or being; not possible.

improvement (im·proov′ mənt) *n.* The state or condition of improving; being improved.

incredible (in·kred′ ə·bəl) *adj.* Hard to believe. *adv.* **incredibly**

inexpensive (in′ ik·spen′ siv) *adj.* Not costly.

insufficient (in′ sə·fish′ ənt) *adj.* Not enough.

investigate (in·ves′ tə·gāt) *v.* To examine closely; to explore.

investigation (in·ves′ tə·gā′ shən) *n.* The careful seeking for facts or information.

irregular (i·reg′ yə·lər) *adj.* Not even or occurring in regular order.

K

knew (noo, nyoo) *v.* Past tense of *to know.*

L

lash (lash) *v.* To tie or fasten. *n.* The cord part of a whip.

last (last) *v.* To go on; to continue for longer than expected. **lasting**

lawbreaker (lô′ brā′ kər) *n.* Someone who breaks the law.

lifeguard (līf′ gärd′) *n.* An expert swimmer who protects and aids other swimmers.

light (līt) *n.* Brightness. *v.* To cause to burn.

live (līv) *adj.* Having life; living.

live (liv) *v.* To be alive; to exist.

M

mailbox (māl′ boks′) *n.* A box in which mail is put.

maintain (mān·tān′) *v.* To carry on; to continue.

match (mach) *v.* To be equal to. *n.* A stick used to light fires.

microfilm (mī′ krə·film) *n.* Thin, flexible photographic material on which printed information is reproduced in very small size.

microscope (mī′ krə·skōp) *n.* An instrument that uses a lens, or combination of lenses, for use in making small objects look larger.

minor (mī′ nər) *adj.* (1) Not very important. (2) Small.

minority (mə·nor′ i·tē) *n.* The lesser part of a whole; smaller number.

misread (mis·rēd′) *v.* To read wrongly.

mistreat (mis·trēt′) *v.* To treat badly.

monstrous (mon′ strəs) *adj.* Unusually large; enormous.

monthly (munth′ lē) *adv.* Every month; once each month.

N

navigate (nav′ i·gāt′) *v.* (1) To follow a course through, on, or over. (2) To direct the course of or operate something, such as an aircraft or ship.

navigation (nav′ i·gā′ shən) *n.* The act or practice of navigating.

navigator (nav′ i·gā′tər) *n.* One who navigates a ship or aircraft.

new (noo, nyoo) *adj.* Having existed only a short time; recently made, produced, or invented.

normal (nôr′ məl) *adj.* Agreeing with or used as an accepted pattern or type; usual. *adv.* **normally**

O

observation (ob′ zər·vā′ shən) *n.* The act of examining and noting facts.

observatory (əb·zûr′ və·tôr′ ē) *n.* A place where scientists use telescopes to study the planets and stars.

obstinate (ob′ stə·nit) *adj.* Stubborn.

obtain (əb·tān′) *v.* To get; to gain. *adj.* **obtainable**

occupy (ok′ yə·pī′) *v.* To live within.

opportunity (op′ ər·tōō′ ni·tē) *n.* A good chance.

orbit (ôr′ bit) *v.* To move in a path around a central body; to revolve. **orbiting**

outlive (out·liv′) *v.* To live longer than.

outrun (out·run′) *v.* To run farther or faster than.

outweigh (out·wā′) *v.* To weigh more than.

overhead (ō′ vər·hed′) *adv.* Above.

overheat (ō′ vər·hēt′) *v.* To heat too much.

oversleep (ō′ vər·slēp′) *v.* To sleep too long.

P

painful (pān′ fəl) *adj.* Full of pain; hurting.

paintbrush (pānt′ brush′) *n.* A brush for applying paint.

panicky (pan′ ik·ē) *adj.* Full of fear.

peace (pēs) *n.* Freedom from war and fighting.

perilous (per′ ə·ləs) *adj.* Full of danger.

periscope (per′ i·skōp) *n.* An instrument in a submarine for viewing objects on the surface of the water.

permanent (pur′ mə·nənt) *adj.* Continuing; intended to last without change.

persuade (pər·swād′) *v.* To urge someone to do something by appealing to his or her feelings. **persuaded, persuading**

piece (pēs) *n.* A separated or broken part; a fragment.

pitch (pich) *v.* (1) To fall forward. (2) To throw something. *n.* Sticky tar.

play (plā) *v.* To have fun. *n.* (1) A story acted out. (2) One's turn in a game.

pollute (pə·lōōt′) *v.* To make dirty or impure. **polluted**

pollution (pə·lōō′ shən) *n.* The act or process of polluting.

portable (pôr′ tə·bəl) *adj.* Able to be carried; easily carried.

post (pōst) *n.* (1) An upright support or marker. (2) A job or position. (3) A system for mail delivery.

pound (pound) *v.* To hit heavily. *n.* (1) A unit of weight. (2) A place for keeping stray animals.

precise (pri·sīs′) *adj.* Clearly defined, accurate.

precision (pri·sizh′ ən) *n.* State or quality of being precise; accuracy.

predict (pri·dikt′) *v.* To declare ahead of time what is going to happen.

prefix (prē′ fiks) *n.* A word part added at the beginning of a root word to form a new word.

preservative (pri·zûr′ və·tiv) *n.* Anything that prevents change or spoilage.

preserve (pri·zûrv′) *v.* To keep from changing or rotting. **preserved**

prey (prā) *n.* Animal hunted and killed for food.

probable (prob′ ə·bəl) *adj.* Likely but not certain to occur or be true.

probably (prob′ ə·blē) *adv.* Very likely.

proof (prōōf) *n.* Evidence that is so clear and final that there is not doubt.

provisions (prə·vizh′ əns) *n.* A stock of supplies, such as food and drink.

punch (punch) *n.* A drink made of fruit juices. *v.* To hit with a fist.

pursue (pər·sōō′) *v.* To chase. **pursued**

Q

quench (kwench) *v.* To satisfy; to put an end to. **quenching**

quietly (kwī′ it·lē) *adv.* In a quiet way.

R

rancher (ran′ chər) *n.* Someone who owns or takes care of a ranch.

recover (ri·kuv′ ər) *v.* To get back something lost or stolen; to regain. **recovered**

recovery (ri·kuv′ ə·rē) *n.* An act of recovering or being recovered.

refer (ri·fûr′) *v.* To relate to; to make a connection or an association with. **referred**

reference (ref′ ər·əns) *n.* Connection; relation.

remark (ri·märk′) *v.* To say or write briefly as a comment; to mention. **remarked**

remarkable (ri·mär′ kə·bəl) *adj.* (1) Unusual; special. (2) Worthy of notice or likely to be noticed.

remit (ri·mit′) *v.* To send, usually money, as in payment.

represent (rep′ ri·zent′) *v.* To speak or act for.

representative (rep′ ri·zen′ tə·tiv) *n.* One who is chosen to represent another or others.

reputation (rep′ yə·tā′ shən) *n.* General knowledge or feeling about someone or something; the opinion or regard of others.

resemblance (ri·zem′ bləns) *n.* Likeness; similarity in looks.

resemble (ri·zem′ bəl) *v.* To look similar to.

reside (ri·zīd′) *v.* To live in or at for a long time; to live officially in one place.

resist (ri·zist′) *v.* To keep from doing.

resistance (ri·zis′ təns) *n.* The act of resisting.

reveal (ri·vēl′) *v.* To make known; to show. **revealed, revealing**

revision (ri·vizh′ ən) *n.* The act or process of changing, improving, or updating.

right (rīt) *adj.* Correct; accurate.

row (rō) *n.* A series of things or people arranged in a line; a line.

row (rou) *n.* A noisy quarrel or fight.

ruins (rōō′ ins) *n.* Remains of something destroyed or decayed.

S

sail (sāl) *n.* A piece of canvas or other material attached to a vessel so as to spread to the wind and cause the vessel to move through the water.

sale (sāl) *n.* Offering or selling of goods at reduced prices.

seclusion (si·klōō′ zhən) *n.* An act of secluding, or shutting oneself away from others.

seize (sēz′) *v.* To take hold of forcibly and suddenly.

seizure (sē′ zhər) *n.* The act of seizing.

sense (sens) *n.* The mental or emotional ability to feel or understand.

sharpen (shar′pən) *v.* To make or become sharp or sharper.

shipwreck (ship′ rek′) *n.* Destruction or loss of a ship.

sickness (sik′ nis) *n.* Condition of being unwell.

sidewalk (sid′ wôk) *n.* A paved path for walking.

silken (sil′ kən) *adj.* Made of silk.

skyscraper (skī′ skrā′ pər) *n.* A very tall building.

skyward (skī′ wərd) *adv.* Toward or in the direction of the sky.

sleepless (slēp′ lis) *adj.* Without or lacking sleep.

slip (slip) *v.* (1) To slide suddenly. (2) To move quietly. (3) To make a mistake.

softness (sôft′ nis) *n.* The condition of being soft.

sole (sōl′) *adj.* Being the only one; only.

solely (sōl′ lē) *adv.* Without any other; singly; alone.

solitude (sol′ i·tōōd′, ·tyōōd) *n.* State of being alone; being away from others.

some (sum) *adj.* Being a certain, not specific number or amount.

species (spē′ shēz) *n.* A kind or type; class.

spell (spel) *n.* (1) A period of work. (2) A period of time. (3) A magic charm.

steal (stēl) *v.* To take the property of another secretly and without permission or right.

steel (stēl) *n.* A hard, strong alloy of iron mixed with a small amount of carbon.

storeroom (stor′ rōōm′) *n.* A room in which things are stored.

subside (səb·sīd′) *v.* To calm or quiet down.

sufficient (sə·fish′ ənt) *adj.* As much as needed or necessary; enough. *adv.* **sufficiently**

suffix (suf′ iks) *n.* A word part added to the end of a root word to form a new word.

sum (sum) *n.* The result obtained from addition.

sunburn (sun′ bûrn′) *n.* Irritation of the skin from being in the sun too long.

suspend (sə·spend′) *v.* To hang down; to hold in place. **suspended**

suspension (sə·spen′ shən) *n.* The state of hanging or being suspended.

T

tail (tāl) *n.* The rear end of an animal's body, forming a distinct movable part that extends beyond the backbone.

tale (tāl) *n.* A story or account of an event or series of events.

tear (tār) *v.* To pull apart, split, or separate into peices.

tear (tēr) *n.* A drop of fluid from the eye.

telegraph (tel′ ə·graf′) *n.* A system, process, or equipment used for sending messages over a distance by means of coded electrical impulses.

telephone (tel′ ə·fōn′) *n.* A system for sending and receiving sound or voice messages over distances.

telescope (tel′ ə·skōp) *n.* An instrument that uses a lens for making distant objects appear nearer and larger.

televise (tel′ ə·vīz′) *v.* To broadcast by television.

television (tel′ ə·vizh′ ən) *n.* An instrument that displays distant images and sounds on a viewing screen.

their (thâr) *adj.* Possessive form of *they*.

there (thâr) *adv.* At or in that place.

timetable (tīm′ tā′ bəl) *n.* A schedule showing the times of events.

too (tōō) *adv.* (1) Also; in addition; besides. (2) More than enough.

toothache (tōōth′ āk′) *n.* An ache or pain in a tooth.

transmit (trans·mit′, tranz·) *v.* To send or cause to go from one person or place to another. **transmitting**

transport (trans·pôrt′) *v.* To bring from one place or person to another.

treacherous (trech′ ər·əs) *adj.* Dangerous; hazardous.

trunk (trungk) *n.* (1) A big box in which items may be stored. (2) The main stem of a tree. (3) The long snout of an elephant.

two (tōō) *n.* The cardinal number that is one more than one.

U

undercook (un′ dər·kŏŏk′) *v.* Cook too little.

underfed (un′ dər·fed′) *v.* Fed too little.

underground (un′ dər·ground′) *adj.* Below ground.

unique (yŏŏ·nēk′) *adj.* Unusual; highly uncommon; rare. *adv.* **uniquely**

V

venture (ven′ chər) *v.* To take a chance to do something that involves risk or danger. **ventured**

venturesome (ven′ chər·səm) *adj.* Willing to take risks; daring.

violence (vī′ ə·ləns) *n.* Great physical force used to cause injury or harm.

violent (vī′ ə·lənt) *adj.* With uncontrolled force.

visionary (vizh′ ə ner′ē) *adj.* of the nature of a vision; illusory.

W

wake (wāk) *v.* To stop sleeping. *n.* A trail left by a ship.

wary (war′ ē) *adj.* Careful.

washable (wosh′ ə·bəl) *adj.* Able to be washed.

watchdog (woch′ dog′) *n.* A dog kept to guard a house.

weak (wēk) *adj.* Lacking strength.

weather (weth′ ər) *n.* The general condition of the atmosphere at a particular time or place.

weekly (wēk′ lē) *adv.* Every week; once each week.

westward (west′ wərd) *adv.* Toward or in the direction of the west.

whether (hweth′ ər) *conj.* A word used to introduce the first of two choices.

whole (hōl) *adj.* Having all of its parts; complete; entire.

wind (wind) *n.* Air in motion.

wind (wīnd) *v.* To turn.

wisely (wīz′ lē) *adv.* In a sensible, intelligent way.

witness (wit′ nis) *n.* One who has personally seen something. **witnessed**

wood (wŏŏd) *n.* Hard, fibrous material beneath the bark of a tree or shrub.

wooden (wŏŏd′ ən) *adj.* Made of wood.

woolen (wŏŏl′ ən) *adj.* Made of wool.

would (wŏŏd) *v.* Past tense of *will.*

write (rīt) *v.* To mark or form letters or words on a surface, as with a pen or pencil.

Y

yellowish (yel′ ō·ish) *adj.* Somewhat like yellow.

Word and Word Part List

Vocabulary Drills, Introductory

Word	Lesson	Word	Lesson	Word	Lesson
-able	12	brighten	20	definitely	9
accomplish	19	calculate	27	destruction	5
accomplishment	R 17–20	calculator	R 25–28	determine	R 9–12
accumulated	17	casual	R 21–24	detest	3
accumulation	R 17–20	casually	23	detestable	R 1–4
accurate	5	catch	6	differ	3
accurately	R 5–8	caution	R 5–8	difference	R 1–4
achieve	R 17–20	cautious	7	differently	R 1–4
admit	24	cents	22	dis-	10
agreement	20	checkbook	8	disaster	15
allege	R 13–16	childish	12	disastrous	R 13–16
alleged	13	close	26	disconnect	10
amass	R 17–20	close	26	dishonest	10
amazement	20	cloudless	12	dishwasher	8
analogy	14	compact	R 17–20	dislike	R 1–4
appointed	19	compacted	17	disprove	10
appointment	R 17–20	composed	11	does	26
assistance	7	composition	R 9–12	does	26
assistant	R 5–8	concealed	7	domestic	2
assured	11	concealing	R 5–8	dove	26
assuring	R 9–12	concluded	9	dove	26
ate	22	conclusion	R 9–12	driftwood	8
authorities	1	confidence	R 5–8	duck	6
authorize	R 1–4	confident	7	dwell	1
balance	4	constructed	9	dwelling	R 1–4
bank	4	construction	R 9–12	eight	22
bass	26	consulted	11	-en	20
bass	26	convince	R 9–12	endure	R 13–16
bay	4	correct	R 25–28	enduring	13
believable	12	crash	6	enough	R 13–16
blaze	4	creak	22	eventual	R 17–20
blew	22	creek	22	eventually	17
blue	22	curable	12	evidence	7
bow	26	dangerous	12	evident	R 5–8
bow	26	dare	R 25–28	excitement	20
brake	22	daybreak	8	exist	R 13–16
break	22	decide	R 9–12	existence	13
break	4	definite	R 9–12	extinct	17